# Choose Joy, Beloved

*Out of a Mother's Grief
into the Father's Arms*

Kathleen Basehore

ISBN 978-1-0980-8803-3 (paperback)
ISBN 978-1-0980-8908-5 (digital)

Christian Faith Publishing, Inc.
832 Park Avenue
Meadville, PA 16335
www.christianfaithpublishing.com

Printed in the United States of America

I dedicate this book to two people. First, to my mother, Barbara Eisenbrown. Mom, you have shown me what persistent strength looks like. I thank you for your example of persevering through hard things. You have been a stronger role model to me than you know.

Second, I dedicate our story to my husband, John, who has been my rock of support and comfort. We have been through the worst of fires and have come out on the other side because of God's grace. Your love has held me steady, especially since Kelsi moved to heaven. You are the biggest blessing in my life.

I love you both.

Kathi

# FOREWORD

$\sim$

B eing asked to write a foreword is an incredible honor. The author has labored for months, sometimes years to craft words that can adequately contain their thoughts, express their emotions, and convey their meaning not only to friends who know and love them but also to strangers they have never met. Writing is deeply personal, and sharing what you have written with the world is incredibly brave.

Publishing a book is a daunting process, and though many embark, few make it to the finish line. I know because much of my life's work has been dedicated to helping authors through this extraordinary journey. It changes you. As the story develops, you learn things about yourself you did not know. You learn things about life, love, and God.

In my writing seminars, I remind people that He (Jesus) is *the* Word of God, but they are *a* Word of God, an epistle not written with hands, that their tongue is the pen of a ready writer, and that in sharing their story—revealing their pain without any polish—they allow their readers permission to explore and share their stories too.

Kathi is one of "my" authors. We first met when she attended one of my Release the Writer seminars. Like many in the room, she had a story to tell—a story she *needed* to tell—but was unsure if telling it would be wise. As a psychologist, how would those in her professional realm react to a story filled with supernatural occurrences? What would happen if she was vulnerable enough to process her internal struggles of coping with parenting an autistic child? What if people mocked her or didn't believe her? What if telling Kelsi's story somehow violated Kelsi? Could she *really* understand? Was it fair to make her autism public?

These are hard questions, and Kathi grappled with them all with a sincere desire to respond to God's call to write her first book, *Can You Just... Love Her?*, in a way that honored Him, protected Kelsi, and offered encouragement to others who parent special needs children. I am so glad she answered the call. Her memoir is a beacon of hope.

I never met Kelsi in person, but I feel as though I got to know her through the pages of Kathi's first book. I wrapped my heart around her and felt a deep connection. My respect for Kathi grew and grew as I read each chapter. I was challenged to place my children more firmly in God's hands. I received the gift of perspective and began to look at things in my life through a different lens.

Kathi and I kept in touch after her book was published, and I knew things were getting harder with Kelsi. She was hurting herself, and things were escalating. I honestly did not know how difficult it had become until I began to read this book, *Choose Joy, Beloved*. As I read more, my heart squeezed in anguish. I could not imagine walking beside my child through the valley in which Kelsi found herself—trauma after trauma, unrelenting, unforgiving, a life under siege.

When I first learned that Kelsi had moved to heaven and the traumatic way that occurred, I sat in stunned silence. I wasn't sure if reaching out to Kathi was the right thing or the wrong thing. I knew from my own trauma that sometimes, the social contract requiring us to respond to well-wishers could be overwhelming. So I wrestled. I wrapped her in prayers and sent a short text. My friend who has counseled so many parents through grief was now grieving.

I marvel at her strength to share her process while it is yet fresh.

This book touches me in a new way. It reveals growth, depth, new realms of grace and understanding—the rest of God, as Kathi put it, "where we may enjoy an indissoluble relationship with Him."

In my life, my deepest understanding and richest growth have always come through suffering. This seems common to man, some-how linked "that I may know Him, and the power of His resurrection, and the fellowship of His sufferings, being made conformable unto His death" (Philippians 3:10 KJV). It is a mystery I have not unraveled, but inherently, I am aware that to taste His resurrection power requires embracing the fellowship of His suffering.

I think Kathi knows this too. In choosing joy through grief, she has touched the resurrection power only available through suffering's fellowship. She has found God in her past, protecting her; God in her present, engaging her; God in her future, inviting her. The valley of the shadow holds treasures too. Our rational minds struggle to embrace this, but our spiritual minds know it to be true.

All of us have experienced grief and trauma, perhaps at different levels, perhaps in different ways, but we have all tasted the bitter broth of loss. Kathi's story will touch your heart. Choose the joy of the Lord, and you get to step into the supernatural strength only this choice can provide.

Wendy K. Walters
wendykwalters.com

# INTRODUCTION

To everything there is a season, and a time for every
matter or purpose under heaven…a time to weep and a
time to laugh, a time to mourn and a time to dance.

—Ecclesiastes 3:1,4 AMP

I present this book, my most painful story ever, for your edification
and comfort. The earliest chapters were the most painful to write.
The rest flowed from time spent in God's presence. After I sent the
manuscript in for publication, God spoke.

"Kathi, you are in a season of grief and tactics" was what I heard.
I wondered how the grief would further manifest after all the healing
He had provided. I knew He would give me the necessary spiritual
combat tactics as defensive weapons. His wraparound presence was
my greatest shield, but now more grief came. He showed me that I
needed regulated times of release of pain after the horrific immediate
months of travail. The brain shifts in hormone production during
shorter but intense episodes and thus reduces the perception of pain.
I looked to Jesus for comfort after these episodes.

The events have often taken me by surprise. A friend sent me
lyrics she had written about Jesus being our blanket in the storm. It
hit me that He had covered me with His presence, and it felt like a
blanket the first day Kelsi moved home to heaven. As I took communion, I realized afresh that His blood is working right here and now. I
cried as a fresh wave of pain escaped my being. I applied His precious
blood to my past, present, and future because God is outside our

time line. He may enter it at any place in time to bring healing. He often uses those closest to us to initiate these moments. I was awed how Jesus moves through His body in tremendous ways.

Another morning, I prayed that God would "change things up today." God loves to do things differently, and I yielded to the Holy Spirit's nudge to request this. He spoke one word to me during the day.

"Italy," He said. I researched current news on Italy and prayed for His kingdom to manifest there in greater ways. A few years before, I had been interested in taking a trip to Italy and wondered why. I have no Italian heritage. On this day, when God spoke about His beloved country, I prayed. It was fun to partner with Him, and I thought that was all there was to it.

Within one day, another friend told me she felt "strongly impressed by God" to send me a video of Italy while a singer sang "Volare." I loved watching the video and listening to the haunting melody. Suddenly, I began to sob, thinking of how Kelsi and I used to travel together. She would have enjoyed such a trip with her whole heart. As the panoramic scenes unfolded and the singer continued to croon, I cried with deep pain until the end. The loneliness I felt was immense. Talking with my husband about our shared pain helped to alleviate most of it.

The next day, my friend said she looked up the words of this song. "*Volare* means to fly, and *cantare* means to sing. I feel like this is how God brings us to joy," she explained. She did not know about the title of this book. My Creator gave me another kiss of His shalom, His peace. The Hebrew concept of peace embraces the promises of good health, prosperity, and peace of mind.

Loss must be felt, embraced, and handed over to the Lord Jesus Christ. God works with us in times and seasons as Ecclesiastes teaches us. For a season, a cycle of time, I knew I would be in this new place of grief. While it would no longer consume me, it would come forth in order to further release smaller bombs of pain still resident in my soul. More comfort came forth with each excruciating bursts. There is no way around it. We must make time to grieve. It is the way through to soar and sing. It takes us back to our joy-giver, the Lord Jesus Christ. Praise Him!

# ONLY THE JOY OF THE
# LORD BRINGS STRENGTH

Take a journey from grief to joy in Kathi Basehore's new book, *Choose Joy, Beloved*. Kathi and her twenty-nine-year-old daughter, Kelsi, had a unique mother-daughter bond. Kelsi dealt with a form of autism that caused her to act out in various ways that would result in harming herself. Both she and Kathi, though, realized the very real spiritual forces at work in Kelsi. She heard clearly from God but also fought real demonic forces.

Kelsi's insight into the spirit realm was a kind of glue that brought her and her mother together in a special bond. For Kathi, a Spirit-filled psychologist, Kelsi was not a patient. She was her only daughter whom she loved and had great hopes for her future. All that ended in a tragic accident.

Kathi relives the extreme depths of grief she went through and passive suicidal desires until the day when she says, "In obedience, I asked God to kindle His passion in me in the middle of the horrendous pain." She says God had told her, "Grief consumes. Keep your eyes on Me… I am here to glue you to all that I am."

Part of her journey from the time her daughter went to her heavenly home was to declare every day, "I choose joy." Don't miss this moving story of how this brokenhearted mother realized only the joy of the Lord could bring her the strength and endurance she needed to continue living each day in victory. If you have a friend walking through the pain of losing a child, this book would speak to them and touch them in ways you never could.

# CHAPTER 1

# My Beautiful Girl

I don't know how he knows it already—
to make art out of messy storms.

—Ann Voskamp

There she lay, sprawled out on the macadam parking lot of her job site. Her head was down as she hopelessly cried. She threw her hands up beseechingly toward her two supervisors who stood about thirty feet away from her. She was begging for understanding, for another chance to be heard. They weren't having any of it. I took all of this in as I drove slowly right next to her and rolled down my window.

"Kelsi, get inside, honey," I said.

Immediately and with relief, she clambered up and fell into the passenger-side seat. She couldn't even speak. My heart broke again for her. Now the supervisors approached my window. They wanted to make sure I knew it wasn't their fault.

They didn't get it. I wasn't ever looking to blame anyone for my daughter's problems. I was just hopeful that she could have a shot at life. Things began to unravel when her OCD (obsessive compulsive disorder) symptoms went into hyperdrive again. What she experienced not even a seasoned adult with OCD could have endured.

I don't remember what I said. We drove away, and Kelsi began to cry and explain. I reached across and held her hand.

"Kelsi, it's okay. It's not your fault. You won't be returning there. You gave it your best shot, and I'm proud of you. Now just lean back and relax," I encouraged her.

Immediately, Kelsi stopped crying, and her head fell back onto the headrest. She slept the rest of the car ride home.

How had we gotten here?

Psalm 116 in the Amplified Bible speaks so well to my life. It is a "how-to" on handling stress and trauma. I use first-person terminology in quoting this because that is how I talk to God.

"I love You, Lord, because You hear my voice and my supplications. Because You have inclined Your ear to me, therefore will I call upon You as long as I live. The cords and sorrows of death were around me, and the terrors of Sheol had laid hold of me; I suffered anguish and grief. Then I called upon Your name: O Lord, I beseech You, save my life and deliver me! Lord, You are gracious, righteous and merciful. You preserve the simple, like me; I was brought low, and You helped and saved me. Return to your rest, O my soul, for the Lord has dealt bountifully with me. God, You have delivered my life from death, my eyes from tears, and my feet from stumbling and falling. I will walk before You, Lord, in the land of the living. I believed and therefore have I spoken, I am greatly afflicted. I said in my haste, all men are deceitful and liars. What shall I render to You for all Your benefits toward me? I will lift up the cup of salvation and deliverance and call on Your name. I will pay my vows to You, Lord, yes, in the presence of all Your people. *Precious in the sight of the Lord is the death of His saints.* O Lord, truly I am Your servant; I am Your servant, the daughter of Your handmaid; You have loosed my bonds. I will offer to You the sacrifice of thanksgiving and will call on Your Name. I will pay my vows to You, Lord, yes, in the presence of all Your people. In the courts of Your house, in the midst of you, O Jerusalem. Praise You Lord!"

I absolutely know that the Lord Jesus Christ hears my voice. I have suffered sorrow and terror, anguish and grief. He has saved my life. He cannot be other than righteous. His grace and mercy rain down upon me. As you continue to read this book, you will see just how bountifully God has dealt with me. Bountiful means God is bighearted, generous, and unstinting in His support toward us. Understand this about God: He is not miserly, tightfisted, or stingy. I offer daily prayers of thanks and praise to He who saved me. I continue to call on His name and gladly admit that in this book. He is my Savior and King. He gave me the title for this book, just as He did for my first one.

I wrote a memoir about raising Kelsi which was published on Mother's Day in 2017. It detailed our lives together as Kelsi battled multiple mental health diagnoses and cognitive impairments. *Can You Just... Love Her?* is available on Amazon at https://www.amazon.com/Can-You-Just-Love-Her/dp/0998956007/. Without question, both tormenting and peacekeeping supernatural forces were at work during Kelsi's entire life. Don't sanitize Christianity. Angels and demons are real.

My memoir ended on a very optimistic note. Kelsi had obtained this job. Her mental health was stable.

When Kelsi saw the completed book, she asked if I would mind if she read it. I laughed and said there would be no book without her. I will always remember her beautiful smile as she received her own copy.

Kelsi held her job for one and a half years. The first few months of her employment were good. She enjoyed her job and the sense of independence that came with it. She came home via public transportation. She talked to everyone on her bus. She would enter our house, glad about her day and proud of accomplishing something. She had three debilitating diagnoses, not counting the cognitive impairments.

The first was Pervasive Developmental Disorder Not Otherwise Specified (PDD-NOS), best understood as a type of autism. Obsessive-Compulsive Disorder (OCD) and Attention Deficit Disorder (ADD) were the other two major ones. OCD and ADD began to get worse. It became more and more difficult for Kelsi to focus, receive, and understand correction on the job.

The easiest way to explain PDD-NOS is to say it is like autism but less severe. Kelsi did not exhibit many of the more typical autistic behaviors, but she had difficulty with reciprocal social interaction and communication skills. She was accepted into the autism waiver program in PA because of having this diagnosis, but I never saw this as her major problem area.

Kelsi was principally affected by spirits of anger, self-hate, and rebellion within the PDD-NOS category.[1]

People who suffer with OCD show symptoms in various categories. The key is how much time the person spends either thinking about what bothers them or trying to avoid it through various compulsive behaviors. These are used to avert imagined catastrophic things from happening to them or loved ones. It's like the gear shift gets stuck in the brain. The major categories include: fear of germs; general uncleanliness; needing things set up in specific order and getting very upset if that order is changed; hoarding items that others would consider useless; excessive checking and repeating actions; and severe ruminating or continual worrying.

Kelsi feared anything unclean. If she used the bathroom in public, she had to hum loudly and run water in the sink to distract herself from the process of elimination within her own body. If someone else came in to use the facility, it could put her over the edge. Disruption became the norm as these symptoms intensified.

The major common denominator in all the categories of OCD is that there is a root of fear. Doubt, a separate spirit, is part of this picture. This makes sense with the symptom of rechecking. I have both felt and heard these spirits speak in regard to Kelsi. Other spirits involved include abandonment, rejection, and low self-esteem.[2] Just because we do not see evil spirits does not mean they do not exist. They travel down generational lines and cause real physical illness in the body and brain.

Dr. Daniel Amen lists six types of ADD in one book and seven in a revised edition. One may be classic, inattentive, overfocused, temporal lobe, limbic, or ring of fire ADD. It depends on the pre-

---

[1]  Barbie Breathitt. Symptoms/Disease, Breath of the Spirit Ministries, 2006.
[2]  Barbie Breathitt. Symptoms/Disease, Breath of the Spirit Ministries, 2006.

dominant symptoms of the sufferer.[3] Kelsi's behaviors fell into the categories of overfocus and ring of fire. She also had some issues in the other categories. Medications that worked for one subtype were often detrimental to another one.

Spirits that often afflict in this category are doublemindedness, deaf and dumb spirits, and a curse coming down the mother's bloodline.[4] In my bloodline, this was most likely the freemasonry curse.

Kelsi's sense of humor nearly evaporated. I had cherished how quirky she was. She would often give what my niece, Ellie, called "Kelsi-isms." These would be sayings that only Kelsi could come up with. Some will be sprinkled throughout this book.

A few months prior to taking her home from the job, Kelsi had a dream.

"Mom, in my dream this morning, God told me to show more humility to my supervisor, and He said I have a lot to learn. He also separated a demon of anger from my humanity," she said.

She had plenty of reasons for anger from all the otherworldly attacks which began at age five and continued throughout her life. Many times, God set her free from one layer of evil, yet there were always more to contend against. Other times, He instructed her how to work on things that would improve her character, even in the midst of the onslaught. It is not an exaggeration to say it was a miracle that His voice got through to her every time. I don't know if I can convey just how awful her life was during her last two years here. I do know with certainty that God never left her.

"What will happen to me when you die? You have to live a long time, Mom," she would say in fear. I had set up another niece, Abby, to be her trustee, but Kelsi knew how dependent she was upon me for so many things.

My brain was always in overdrive. There was too much going on.

---

[3]  Daniel G. Amen, *Healing ADD: The Breakthrough Program That Allows You to See and Heal the 6 Types of Attention Deficit Disorder* (G. P. Putnam's Sons, 2001).

[4]  Barbie Breathitt. Symptoms/Disease, Breath of the Spirit Ministries, 2006.

"Mom, who's working with me today? What are we going to be doing?" she asked as I was texting a client about a change in appointment time. Quickly after this came a text from her behavior specialist, wanting to know when we could set up the next autism treatment team meeting. Then appointments were made for OT. She joined a dance group which was an hour away from our home. My cell phone rang insistently as another client tried to get through.

"May Patrick and Kayla come up soon, Mom?" These two young adults also had autism and were her best friends.

"I want to go to Unending Promise this week," I groaned, looking at my work schedule. When staff was unavailable, it fell on John and me to meet all her needs. We wanted her to have as full a life as possible, so we drove her to the destinations many times and picked her up.

"Mom, I need you to pray with me."

And I would as soon as possible. Sometimes our prayer times went over an hour.

"Mom, you're too touchy," she said after a head-spinning day. Before I could say anything, she closed her eyes and listened.

"God said, 'Your Mom's had enough today. Don't start a fight, either of you,'" she said.

I almost laughed in the stress. I saw how God desires to help us in every situation every day.

Her OCD escalated until she began to hit herself on the forehead. It started out minimal but progressed in intensity. She loved the beach, but even taking a trip to the ocean did not help. To give her some independence, I got two adjoining hotel rooms. She constantly knocked on our door with questions. She was nervous about being alone, though she was right next door and could come in and out as she pleased.

"When are we going out on the beach?"

"Where is my hotel key?"

"How do you work this TV?"

"Do you have my pills? I don't see them!"

I thought it would be good to walk on the boardwalk. It was not. It was very sad and stressful. She was enraged because the day was overcast and windy.

"What am I supposed to do now? I wanted to go in the ocean! This sucks! There is no sun, and it's cold!"

I silently prayed to God for help. Within a few minutes, the sun emerged and shone intensely the rest of the day. Her mood brightened, but it was still a rough trip. She actually did go in the very cold ocean, and I could not see how she stood to do so.

John and I walked on eggshells most of the time. She became angry and paced. She even posed like a statue. We hadn't seen this behavior since she was very young. Her psychiatrist advised that we stop her current medications. Father's Day rolled around, and John saw her card on the table. She was upstairs, and he opened it. Big mistake.

"What? *You opened it without me watching? No, you can't do that! Do it over!*" she begged.

To stop the meltdown, John quickly put the card back inside and reopened it. With tears in her beautiful eyes, she asked if he liked it, and he assured her he did. Oh, she was in such pain the last two years of her life here. She left the room to talk to God. When she returned, she was peaceful.

"God gets a kick out of me because I'm so changeable," she said.

I saw this was a very different way for me to perceive her behaviors. It helped for me to take God's perspective, as usual. Even in the midst of OCD-fueled tantrums, God gave hope because He knew it was not her fault. One OCD belief was that she had to observe things "perfectly," and since she had missed John opening her card, it created great fear and rage inside. God showed me how to be a better mom in the midst of truly crazy circumstances.

Ann Voskamp, a well-known writer, sends out daily e-mails. She wrote this about creativity:

> I don't know how He knows it already—to make art out of messy storms. The essence of creativity is essentially risk, believing enough to leap

into the yet unseen. The theological term for this is faith. Creativity is good theology; it's what God did in the beginning. When we stop fearing failure, we start being artists. You have to bury your fear in faith. Otherwise, you bury your talents.

I took this to heart. I colored a picture of a lion with the words "Creativity Takes Courage" and posted it on my closet door. Kelsi greatly admired it, so I knew it was from God's spirit inside of me.

As Kelsi's suffering increased in the summer of 2017, I prayed more and made decrees from the Bible.

"What, what would have become of me had I not believed that I would see the Lord's goodness in the land of the living" (Psalm 27:13 AMP).

I always identified strongly with that verse. One day, I stepped outside on my deck. I exalted the name of Jesus and began to make a demand on heaven for Kelsi and for others whom I counselled. I thought of the pain in people's eyes as they told me their stories of loss. I felt the anger of God against the enemy of our souls, who laughs at and loves to inflict pain upon us and our children. I shouted until I had to begin my workday, listening to more brokenhearted people.

That evening, I could not sleep until 2:00 a.m. In despair, I prayed without words. I had a dream.

A man stood before me on a bus which was filled with many people. I recognized him as someone I had worked with many years ago. His name was Art, and he reminded me of Santa Claus.

"How often do you pray like that?" he asked. "Shouting!" Now I observed a twinkle in his eyes.

I put my head down in my hands, recognizing that everyone on the bus now knew I had been shouting in prayer to God that day. "Never," I sadly admitted. I woke up.

I knew this was a God encounter because the dream was very powerful. What was Art's last name? Hey or Hay or something like that? Sudden delighted shock waves went through my brain.

"His last name was High! That's incredible," I said out loud.

"Art High" let me know that he liked my shouting in prayer.

"In the days of His flesh, Jesus offered up definite, special petitions and supplications with strong crying and tears to Him Who was able to save Him from death, and He was heard because of His reverence toward God" (Hebrews 5:7 AMP).

I just prayed like Jesus did when He walked on this earth. Jesus still lives to make intercession for us. I recognized that I now live so He can do this through me. Don't hesitate to make a demand on heaven in prayer.

> Our Christ is risen. He is a living Christ who lives within us. We must not have this truth merely as a theory. Christ must be risen in us by the power of the Spirit. The power that raised Him from the dead must animate us, and as this glorious resurrection power surges through our beings, we will be freed from all our weaknesses... You must learn to take the victory and shout in the face of the devil, "It is done!" There is no man who can doubt if he learns to shout.[5]

Kelsi told me she was more aware of angelic activity all around us, even with the tormenting thoughts that assailed her mind. She also began making her own decrees about her life from the Word of God and felt calmer. She did so well at work on these days her employer thought she would not need support people with her. This is how charged and changeable the spiritual atmosphere was around her.

Then rage hit her, and she blamed me for her symptoms. As we prayed together, she was aware of great bitterness inside. She told Jesus how she felt.

"Confessing it to Him makes it come out like poison. He's taking all of it, and now I need to repent for how I felt toward you. He took the evil out, Mom. I choose to forgive you," she said in relief.

---

[5] Smith Wigglesworth, "The Shout of Faith," *The Master's Healing Presence Bible by Benny Hinn* (Thomas Nelson, 2003), pp. 1167–1167.

God held me so that I could hear her rage, pray with her, and watch Him heal. This was difficult to do but also amazing to witness.

I once heard someone sing, "His blood didn't come cheap, so you gotta go deep." Going deep with Kelsi in prayer was worth it.

Kelsi had difficulty understanding how to receive correction without feeling self-hate. When a bus driver told her not to be late for her pick-up, she became angry because hearing this reinforced her mistake, so she tried to excuse her behavior.

"It's *not my fault* I had to go to the bathroom after work! I wasn't even that late, and the bus driver jumped all over me!" she exploded at home. I would see these behaviors at her autism waiver meetings also. When staff gave her a correction, she went into what I called a "shame spin," and it was impossible to pull her out of it. I learned to have her take a time-out so she could regroup and get away from the stimulation. Later on, I told her what was happening inside, and she learned from it. I would say, "Don't go into a shame spin," and she came out more quickly. It took time to forgive others and more importantly herself at the deepest root where shame sat. People didn't understand that her raging reactions were against herself. She vented out and blamed others, but it was because she was trying to defend herself about being "wrong." It was a very hard place for her to be. I was so proud that she received this understanding from me and did her best to grow from it.

Kelsi's primary defense was to stay in a fantasy realm. It hurt too much to be "here" in the present.

"I don't trust anyone or myself. I don't want to have any more ugly memories. I am sick of living in this mortal world. I would rather live out yonder," she said.

"You mean you'd rather live in a fantasy world?" I asked.

She nodded.

"Kelsi, God's realm is so much more fantastic than fantasy. Don't be afraid. Jesus wants to set all of us free and bring us closer into more freedom and joy. I bet that includes having incredible experiences with Him," I said.

She said she would try to listen but felt a need to protect herself by escaping into her inner world. Then she saw Jesus before her. "He wants me to let go of it and is reminding me of some of the good decrees I said before," she said. As always, she relaxed when she heard His voice.

Kelsi took a weekend trip with her cousin, Abby. They went to Niagara Falls. It was a tough experience for both of them, but they also had some fun. Abby recognized how difficult life was for Kelsi. It was a main reason she resorted to the use of fantasy in her life. It was a well-worn defense mechanism to handle pain.

Several years earlier, I had a dream where I tried to pull Kelsi out of water, but she resisted. She slumped into the water, eyes closed in ecstasy. I pulled her out. She fell back in. It was quite a battle. Evil pummeled her so viciously in her mind. Fantasy was the lure. It promised her great release. She became totally engrossed in movies and talked about the plot and actors as though that was reality. When I corrected her, she responded with anger and denial. She was peaceful with the distraction of movies.

One day, Kelsi said, "Mom, I don't think I should be here."

"Kelsi, God determines your days. He knit your spirit together with your soul in my womb. How can you say you're not supposed to be here?" I asked.

She fell back onto her bed and rolled her eyes in surprise. "You just hit me with truth," she admitted. That was because what I said came out of God's Word.

> For You did form my inward parts; You did knit me together in my mother's womb. I will confess and praise You for You are fearful and wonderful and for the awful wonder of my birth! Wonderful are Your works, and that my inner self knows right well. My frame was not hidden from You when I was being formed in secret (and) intricately and curiously wrought (as if embroidered with various colors) in the depths of the earth (a region of darkness and mystery)" (Psalm 139:13–15 AMP)

I am struck by the phrase "intricately and curiously wrought" in this Psalm. God designed our brains to experience, encapsulate, and manage traumas in life. Kelsi's brain was wired in angry response to frustration from her earliest years. The limbic (emotional) brain circuits operate at a much faster speed than do those of our prefrontal cortex where reasoning rules. Neural integration of these areas is blocked by traumatic childhood experiences. Our brains naturally dissociate from these traumas in order to deal with things that are too horrific for us at the time. We form multiple parts which are soul fragments that hold horror. These remain separate and detached from our functioning identity which must handle everyday life situations such as work and school.

Our functioning identity becomes aware of our unhealed wounds later on as those memories begin to emerge. A person who is a Christian may have childhood parts that do not know Jesus. Separate beliefs may be held by soul fragments within the personality system. Jesus knows all of this and loves to bring healing to us. It is vital that we see ourselves through His eyes in order to connect to such parts with empathy and compassion.

Have you ever said, "A part of me wants to do it and a part of me does not?" This is an easy way to understand that all people are fragmented to some extent.

For example, the freemasonry curse in my bloodline opened a door for unbelief and fear to enter so that I could not fully appropriate that Jesus became that curse for me on the cross. By His grace, He healed me so that I could fully apprehend truth. Jesus heals all fragmentation, and we become whole. We perceive who we were really created to be.

Kelsi understood the parts concept immediately. She was able to do some of the work of integration in prayer with Jesus. More explanation will be found about this in the chapter on trauma. I coached her to see Jesus in the memories with her younger parts. Jesus did amazing things to bring healing as she watched. The result was increased neural integration. In other words, she began to hold her brain in her mind. She learned how to stay present and be engaged with Jesus in the midst of difficult memories.

Emily Dickinson put it this way: "The brain is wider than the sky—for—put them side by side—the one the other will contain with ease—and you—beside."

It is explained that this is the starting point of one of Emily Dickinson's great meditations on the power of human imagination and comprehension.[6]

God created our imaginations as a way to connect with Him. Fantasy becomes a defense mechanism that temporarily soothes the soul but disconnects us from God. We may ask God to heal, lead, and use our imaginations in the perfect way He desires to do so.

Another brain concept is that of mirror neurons. These are brain cells which become activated when we see someone doing something. We then learn by imitating that behavior. For example, we yawn when someone else does. Laughter is contagious as are many other emotions. I recognized something astounding one day. Both Kelsi and I received so much healing directly from Holy Spirit as we communed with Him. He is Spirit, He is the third Person of the Trinity, and He has a mind. His mirror neurons were affecting ours because real lasting change was the result. Just because we could not see Him did not mean we could not receive stability from His thoughts.

More problems ensued. More healing came. The medications Kelsi took contributed to significant weight gain. She reacted with anger and shame when I tried to help her with diet. The day I let go and asked God to help her, He stepped up immediately.

"Mom, God said eating less is key. He said if I don't eat as much, my brain will be less active," she said.

At first, I was speechless. Then awe and worship arose.

"God, I never would have thought to say that to her. You are a genius!" I praised. Only God could motivate her by such wisdom and compassion. I simply needed to let go. That very night, she had more healing.

"God said He's taking a demon out of me, and it came out of the middle of me, all black and shiny. It relaxed me. I felt more at

---

6   https://interestingliterature.com/2017/11/a-short-analysis-of-emily-dickinsons-the-brain-is-wider-than-the-sky/

ease," she explained later. A second encounter involved Jesus pulling out a long black thing from her brain that was connected into the earth.

"God just said, 'That's the thing about the spirit world. Something huge can be inside of you that's connected into the earth.' You're lucky you can't see this. It's gross," she finished.

I could sense this was not her use of fantasy. God was truly showing her something from His realm. I prayed and asked God to fill her up with His peace. Her behaviors changed to such a positive and significant degree after these encounters that I believed God intervened. In other words, if it was a psychotic experience, she would not have come to such peace. Character change was the result.

Kelsi talked to God at work when the pressure became too much. She said her supervisor called her "spoiled." All this did was contribute to the self-hate inside. People just didn't understand. She asked God why she was even alive.

"It's hard on you, but I will always have a bubble over you. Pray to Me to cover you from negative words and then be positive. Think of Me and pray. Think of a good, happy, or silly song," she heard Him say. I then pulled off the "spoiled" label in prayer and asked God to wash away all shame attached to it. Kelsi forgave her boss.

Kelsi feared losing her job. More instances of behavior problems happened, and shame increased. To engage with shame, one must continue to develop resilience in order to get to the places of vulnerability inside. Kelsi's capacity for this was greatly eroded.

For the first time, Kelsi began to talk of the beauty of heaven. She had always wanted a life here on earth, but the stress was now too much. She hit herself harder on the forehead.

"I feel horribly mangled. I haven't been able to keep a job. It's ridiculous," she cried. As we prayed, she heard God tell her she is in Christ, a new creation, and she should not feel shame about herself at all.

"I'm a new creation with new problems," she retorted.

"You may have new problems, but I'm not exhausted to tangle with them with you. Your parents love you, Kelsi," God told her. Kelsi felt we overprotected her. Suddenly, she shifted.

"I yield my brain to Jesus," she said.

"It's starting to clear up inside." She bent over. "Wow," she said as she felt peace again.

Although many difficult things were happening, I was aware of personal growth. I no longer felt pressured about time. I was able to flow with whatever the day presented. God counselled me to choose laughter one day. Within a few minutes, I heard sounds of loud merriment from Kelsi's room.

"What's so funny?" I called to her.

"I'm laughing with God, Mom, He just tweaked my nose," she said. This happened all the time. God would speak to me and manifest at the same time in Kelsi.

Yet the fear of uncleanliness became worse. OCD will morph if left unchecked, and Kelsi had difficulty "checking" it. When she saw cat litter on a cartoon, she refused to go to her day program. Her worker went home. I was exhausted, so I lay down. Immediately, I felt four strong taps on my inner elbow. Nobody was with me in the room.

"Get up!" I heard in my mind. I began to pray and became energized. God often directly intervened like this. I was so aware of God's ever-present presence in every messy moment.

In my journal, I wrote, "Life is crazy now. Kelsi's stress is so high, and I am worn out. The enemy wants to wear me down, but I still feel so grateful to God!" We continued to pray together, and Kelsi always received some measure of healing, but full restoration of her mind did not occur. We welcomed all moments of respite.

There is an area in your brain called the joy center. Unlike some other areas of the brain that go through pruning, neurons here continue to grow until you die. This is good news for all who have gone through hard things. Resilience is defined as the ability to recover strength, spirits, and good humor quickly. A synonym is buoyancy which is lightness of spirit. In other words, resilience is the ability to come back to joy. This is extremely important.

One time, I saw a mother show her son how to return to joy. She corrected his rambunctious behavior in a doctor's office. The little boy covered his face in his hands and walked away from her. She then gently patted the sofa cushion next to her and encouraged him to come sit with her. He did, and the recovery to joy on his face was a beautiful thing to see.

If an adult did not show you how to do this as a child, don't despair. Ask God to teach you about this pathway. He may take you there directly as you focus on Him. He may do it through connection with loving people around you. Either way, you can get there and abide in the one who is joy.

I knew God was leading us to follow the pathway back to joy in our brains. God can do anything. With the Joy-Giver inside us, the path to joy can be established no matter what trials we experience. It's a miracle. We are to learn to focus on positive things which results in changes to our brains.

> Finally, brothers, whatever is true, whatever is noble, whatever is right, whatever is pure, whatever is lovely, whatever is admirable—if anything is excellent or praiseworthy—think about such things. Whatever you have learned or received or heard from me, or seen in me—put it into practice. And the God of peace will be with you. (Philippians 4:8, 9 NIV)

We would need God's presence more than ever over the next two years.

# CHAPTER 2

# A Sharper Descent

The tree of life must grow in your brain to replace
the tree of knowledge. Sometimes it hurts.

—God

Things went from bad to worse.

"Mom! Go outside and clean up the deck rail! There's stuff on it!" Kelsi hit her forehead harder, ran inside the house, and got paper towels and Windex.

"I'll do it, honey," I said as I tried to intercept her. I gasped when I saw how hard she was now hitting herself. Far be it for us to say the words "bird poop" or "pee" because that sent her into a greater frenzy of head-hitting. Toilet bowls always had to be closed or she would spit in the bathroom. Other words became unacceptable as they attached to distressing thoughts which covered the unclean area.

"What's going on?" John came upstairs with all the racket.

"I have to clean off the deck from bird deposits," I said.

"No, don't say that word! How could you do that? Now I have to hit myself!" Kelsi would yell and run from the room, often spitting on the way. She now associated the word *deposits* with "poop and pee." There was such strong control around this it was exhausting. We could not be careful enough.

One day, something shifted inside of me. I felt a strong desire for a dog again. After our last two dogs died, we decided to live pet-free. Kelsi had adjusted to them but would avoid watching them go to the bathroom outside. At this stage, Kelsi did not want me to get one. I am still so surprised that in spite of Kelsi's rage with "deposits" that I decided to get a dog anyway. It took a lot of negotiation as we discussed how we would handle the bathroom issues. We felt we could usually keep things out of her sight since our yard is quite large. I even discerned that God was in this desire for a pet.

The morning I arranged to meet the breeder halfway for the exchange, Kelsi began yelling upstairs. She even said she felt suicidal. I knew it was supernatural, so I hung up the phone and went toward her. I needed to address some kind of spirit but did not know until I got closer to her.

"Chaos, I rebuke you in Jesus's name. Come off her right now!" I commanded. Sometimes you must move toward evil in order to disempower it. It was not the first time God required me to take action without knowing what was manifesting. As always, He was faithful to reveal what was needed. Kelsi went from rage to immediate calm. I saw her eyes clear up. I explained what our plan was for the day, and she was fine with it.

We picked up our new mini-Siberian Husky and brought her home. God told me her name was Zoe, which means abundant life. I knew it helped that I had to call out her name so many times every day as I trained her. I released the life of God every time I spoke it. Kelsi avoided her most of the time, but the moments when they enjoyed each other were beautiful.

The stress at home increased. At times, Kelsi and I got very angry with each other. I was overextended with training Zoe, so I didn't handle her anger as well as before. She usually ran to my sister's house for a while and then cooled down. That happened a few times. As much stress as we experienced, I was amazed it was not more often.

God helped Kelsi with Zoe as with everything else that bothered her. One time, Zoe grabbed a piece of chicken off of Kelsi's plate. Kelsi yelled at her and would not calm down when I tried to reason with her. Suddenly, she paused and began to chuckle.

"Mom, God just said, 'Why don't you look at it this way? Zoe never gets human food. That was a treat for her.' I never thought of it like that. It's true." God's peace invaded her moment. He always knew exactly what to say to her.

I recognized how controlled I was by this when I took a walk with Zoe. I stopped so some children could pet her. A little girl asked me what was in my "bag" which I carried to pick up bowel movements.

"Those are her deposits," I said.

"You mean her poops?" the little one innocently asked.

I felt relaxed and sad at the same time.

"Yes, I mean her poops," I said.

She smiled and I gratefully acknowledged the freedom in the word. But Kelsi was not allowed that liberty, and when we slipped and said it, hell came calling.

A supernatural intervention began to have a positive impact. This same gift from God helped me through the hardest times of intense grief after Kelsi moved to heaven. This intervention is called speaking in tongues through the power of the Holy Spirit. Jesus promised his disciples the Holy Spirit would come to them after He ascended back into heaven.

> I will ask the Father, and He will give you another Comforter (Counselor, Helper, Intercessor, Advocate, Strengthener and Standby), that He may remain with you for-ever—the Spirit of Truth, Whom the world can-not receive (welcome, take to its heart), because it does not see Him or know and recognize Him. But you know and recognize Him, for He lives with you (constantly) and will be in you. (John 14:16, 17 AMP)

In the book of Acts, chapter 2, the physician Luke records that Jesus showed Himself alive to his disciples and to many other people after He had died on the cross. He did so many times over forty days post-resurrection. He instructed them about the things of the kingdom of God.

And while being in their company and eating at the table with them, He commanded them not to leave Jerusalem but to wait for what the Father had promised, of which (He said) you have heard Me speak. For John baptized with water, but not many days from now you shall be baptized with (placed in, introduced into) the Holy Spirit. (Acts 1:4 5 AMP)

The disciples obeyed Jesus. When the day of Pentecost came, they were all in one place, praying together. The Holy Spirit came with a mighty violent tempest blast, and what appeared to be tongues of fire rested upon the disciples. They began to speak in other languages. Jews from different parts of the world were present at this time because it happened during the Feast of Pentecost, and they were in Jerusalem to celebrate. When they heard the Gospel being spoken in their own native tongue, many believed and were baptized that day.

The gift of tongues is a Holy Spirit prompted ability to pray and praise God in a dialect that may or may not be related to any human language on earth. The syllables or words are understood by Father God, Jesus, and the Holy Spirit but not by the speaker unless God gives them the interpretation.

In 1 Corinthians chapter 14, the Apostle Paul explains that tongues is a form of prayer, praise, and thanksgiving to God. We build ourselves up by speaking in tongues when no one is present. In other words, our spirit is edified though our mind and understanding are not. Holy Spirit bypasses our intellect or cognitive processes when we do this. God may choose to give us the interpretation of what we are praying. For instance, once I prayed in tongues in faith for about two hours. At the very end of that time, my lips formed the phrase "Praise God!" This happened without my control. I assumed that was at least part of the interpretation of my prayer time.

An interesting study was conducted by Dr. Andrew Newberg at the University of Pennsylvania. He wanted to measure brain activity while participants spoke in tongues. The scans revealed that the frontal lobe, the area responsible for language, went "dark." Participants knew words were coming out but were not conscious of what they were saying. This agrees with the Bible which states our minds are not aware during this process. This is in contrast to other religions and faiths that speak a language while in meditation. Here the frontal lobes were active while words were uttered by those subjects. *ABC Nightline* did a feature on this which is available on YouTube.[7]

There are many times I do not know what to pray, and in those moments, I pray in tongues. I do not debate this issue with others because the Holy Spirit has taught me directly the great value of this gift. I do believe that if tongues are spoken within the church body, an interpretation is needed in order to truly edify everyone present.

When the Apostle Paul spoke of his mind being unfruitful, he meant he was not engaging his intellect when he spoke in tongues. He knew there was a very valuable spiritual transaction taking place beyond what his mind could understand. Paul was a highly educated Pharisee of the tribe of Benjamin, and he found this spiritual practice invaluable. I believe this gift is an indispensable aid to functioning effectively here on the earth.

I experienced a strong manifestation of tongues when the Spirit of God first touched me in my bedroom. I felt something hit me on the side of my head, and I jumped out of my chair and began speaking in what felt like a war type of dialect. I did not understand any of the words I was saying. That certainly piqued my curiosity to understand this phenomenon. I studied this gift. It is also important to know that one may receive this gift in faith without experiencing any particular manifestation.

---

[7]  http://robertwimer.com/this-is-what-happens-in-the-brain-when-christians-speak-in-tongues/

After God imparted it to me in my bedroom, I had an opportunity to receive it again when I went to a conference in Texas. The meeting was held by Mr. and Mrs. Hunter, an elderly couple in their nineties who had a very strong healing ministry. When Mr. Hunter stood to ask if any would like to receive this gift, I did so because I felt very safe under him. The next day, I stood at their book table. Mr. Hunter gave a soft cry, took my hand, and pulled me toward himself. He then gave me a kiss on my cheek with fatherly love. I noted that his face actually glowed. It reminded me of the face of Moses who spent much time in God's presence on Mt. Sinai.

> Moses was there with the Lord forty days and forty nights; he ate no bread and drank no water. And he wrote upon the tables the words of the covenant, the Ten Commandments. When Moses came down from Mount Sinai with the two tables of the Testimony in his hand, he did not know that the skin of his face shone and sent forth beams by reason of his speaking with the Lord. (Exodus 34:28, 29 AMP)

I believe this gift is available to any believer in Jesus because of my personal experience. The Holy Spirit is our best teacher. I now pray in my private prayer language to God as often as possible.

God spoke to me about the ability of our minds to "pivot" away from negative thoughts. Psychologists often use a technique called Cognitive Behavioral therapy. The client is taught to identify categories of thinking traps and then refute them. It can be a valuable help for people, but Kelsi was unable to use it, even with the use of psychotropic medications. The assault of lies coming against her mind was simply too strong. When she spoke in tongues, relief came.

Kelsi and I had both received our private prayer language in faith, so I began to urge her to speak in tongues when the thoughts hit. If I could remind her early enough, she would comply. It stopped the distressing flow, and she calmed down.

Shame was an ever-present trigger for Kelsi. I continued to pray with her and explain that our minds are capable of meta-awareness. This means we have a higher ability to observe the processes of our conscious mind and our emotions. We pause and take a step back out of the emotions and observe them. We are then better able to regulate our responses, attention span, and focus. This is helpful to develop more skill in biblical meditation practice. I found it just as helpful to mitigate strong emotional reactions. To recognize one is feeling shame puts it "out there" for your conscious mind to handle. Speak to yourself with empathy. "This is just the emotion of shame. It feels painful but it will pass. I am not bad. I simply feel the pressure and lies of shame." The Word tells us how Jesus dealt with shame.

"Looking to Jesus, the founder and perfecter of our faith, who for the joy that was set before him endured the cross, despising the shame, and is seated at the right hand of the throne of God" (Hebrews 12:2 ESV).

In addition to explaining this to people, I prayed for them to experience being washed clean of shame by the blood of Jesus Christ. This type of prayer brought lasting change to their lives.

I had an encounter while I was resting in bed. I saw and felt a strong presence lay down next to me. I felt it touch my right thigh strongly, pressing down several times. I asked, "Are you from God?"

Suddenly, I had an open-eyed vision. A bright orange swirly light went right by my head.

Kelsi prayed when I told her about it.

"Jesus has you covered, Mom. Nothing can get to you. Just welcome Him," she said.

Within a week, Chuck Pierce, my web church leader, said that God is imparting spiritual energy to us that was His power and glory. This would result in us doing things we normally would not have done before. He said unconventional wisdom was being given. The prophetic word encouraged, strengthened, and edified me.

In spite of the horrendous daily events, I believed Kelsi would be healed of mental illness. I had been believing this for many years.

"Mom, just be still. I like it when we're not rushing around," Kelsi said as she hugged me.

A holy hush enveloped both of us. It felt wonderful. How often did we just stop and rest? It seemed we were always running here or there. More doctor appointments started because of the hitting. More specialists came onboard. Now we were required to keep a tab on how many times she hit herself. I had to record it. It made me crazy. In fact, I just didn't do it. I asked the team to record when they were alone with her. It made it so much worse to have to write everything down, though this was a behavioral approach that they hoped would bring change eventually.

"Mom, I imagined the Holy Spirit kissing me on my forehead. It felt so real, and I chose to believe it. Imagination can be reality. It's the same thing, Mom," she explained.

In spite of the increased turmoil, she still came up with "Kelsi-isms." For example, after I got my hair colored a brighter red, she said, "With your red hair and blue eyes and colorful robe, you look like a happy jellybean of a lady." It made me laugh in the midst of all the hard stuff.

Kelsi would repeat herself or compulsively rewind movies or taped TV shows, watching them over and over. This was usually so she could "see or hear it perfectly." She still wanted to fantasize. She would or could not give that up.

We were just standing in our kitchen, and Kelsi had an open vision about Jesus.

"Whoa, Mom, it's about the blood of Jesus. There's a chain reaction from His sacrifice He made when He died on the cross. It's something about His blood being like a time warp. It's like *Star Trek!* Even though it happened long ago, it heals *now*," she said.

I felt the glory in her words as God gave her this revelation. We praised Him.

As the hitting increased, Kelsi turned to God more.

"I asked God how to become one with Him. He came to me like a cloud. His presence and angels told me it happened because I asked. The angels faded as He came in. He's a person, it's huge, there is a lot to drink from Him! He said he loved me. Suddenly, I wanted to be one with Him. It's like climbing up a steep mountain. I'm not sure how far I can climb and don't feel I have the strength to do it. It's not just physical. It could have a spiritual impact on me. Even more dark things come at me when I advance in it."

I asked her to ask God about what she just said.

"He said when evil brings the dark, we bring the light, and the goodness of all things is in the light. So it will be okay if I ascend the mountain of the Lord. I still want to be one with Him. I just fear I won't have enough energy," she said.

I gave her a long hug, and she commented on how "soft" I felt just then.

Kelsi met a Vietnam veteran one day while reading in the local bookstore. He told her that many veterans committed suicide. This greatly upset her.

"Mom, I had a dream that a storm was coming, and I prayed against the suicides, and God told me it was an amazing prayer," she said. Kelsi always prayed from her heart. It was humbling to discern. I then agreed with her in prayer and commanded the enemy would not be able to retaliate against us.

"Kelsi, it's like that song, 'You Can't Touch This.' The enemy can't touch Jesus," I said. I remember how she laughed. The next day, Chuck Pierce quoted the same song title on his webcast as he extolled the Lord Jesus. I loved when God witnessed to Himself through such confirmations.

Both Kelsi and I experienced God delivering us from evil spirits in our dreams. I still receive healings like this today. I'm not sure how many Christians realize God can and will do this for you. Some Christians don't believe they are influenced by demons. We all are, though we don't know it. We will not be perfect until we are in heaven. That means here on earth, we will continue to need healing. Some of us need more intervention than others, but we are all in need of help. We usually don't even know what we need until God shows us.

"Kathi, the tree of life must grow in your brain to replace the tree of knowledge there," God explained. "Sometimes it hurts," He added.

Kelsi hit a root memory of a preschool teacher knocking on her head, asking if anyone was home. As she forgave that person, she suddenly had insight. Years before in high school, she said something very cruel to a teacher. I tried to explain how bad it was, but she could not digest it because she was so angry at the time. In this moment, pain and sadness shone from her eyes.

"Mom, I can't believe I said that to her! I never meant it! I wouldn't say something so evil to someone!" This was true repentance coming from her heart. She asked God to forgive her. When she obeyed God and forgave the first teacher, He revealed the truth about the vengeance she took upon the second. She was set free to see the truth, repent, and return to God. Forgiveness is powerful and will always result in more self-healing.

"Or do you presume on the riches of His kindness and forbearance and patience, not knowing that God's kindness is meant to lead you to repentance" (Romans 2:4 ESV)?

> Yet I am glad now, not because you were pained, but because you were pained into repentance (that turned you to God); for you felt a grief such as God meant you to feel, so that in nothing you might suffer loss through us or harm for what we did. For Godly grief and the pain God is permitted to direct, produce a repentance that leads and contributes to salvation and deliverance from evil, and it never brings regret; but worldly grief (the hopeless sorrow that is characteristic of the pagan world) is deadly (breeding and ending in death). (2 Cor 7:10 AMP)

When we forgive ourselves and others, we release power from the Holy Spirit inside of us. Jesus said that when we choose not to forgive, the sins of others are held against them. In this case, both the oppressor and oppressed lose. The power of the Holy Spirit cannot be released into the situation to free self or the other. Victim and oppressor remain bonded in an unholy dance.

"If you forgive the sins of anyone, they are forgiven; if you retain the sins of anyone, they are retained" (John 20:23 AMP).

"Then I returned and considered all the oppressions that are practiced under the sun. And I beheld the tears of the oppressed, and they had no comforter; and on the side of their oppressors was power, but they (too) had no comforter" (Ecclesiastes 4:1 AMP).

I am so proud of how humble Kelsi was in receiving healing from God. I was so honored to be her mom and pray with her many times.

Psychology teaches about forgiveness from a humanistic perspective which leaves God out of the equation. Humanism is defined as an outlook or system of thought, attaching prime importance to human rather than divine or supernatural matters. Humanist beliefs stress the potential value and goodness of human beings, emphasize common human needs, and seek solely rational ways of solving human problems.[8]

From a humanist perspective, to believe that forgiveness means forgetting is nonsense. Yet, through the blood of Jesus, God does forget our sin. In fact, we are so cleansed by the sacrifice of Jesus that it's as if we never sinned in the first place. Psychology says you can accept an offense against you without excusing it. God says cry out to Him; give Him your pain and your need for vengeance. Then you will be able to fully excuse the offender. Jesus takes the case for you, and you are no longer laboring under feeling offended. Humanistic thought says forgiveness is not a decision. It is an attitude or habit of mind.

God says we are to forgive others, just as Jesus forgave us while He hung, bloody and unrecognizable, on the cross. He was murdered because He gave Himself for us in obedience to Father God. The truth is forgiveness is a decision in obedience to a holy God. Jesus is King. We are to emulate Him.

"There is no (human) wisdom or understanding or counsel (that can prevail) against the Lord" (Proverbs 21:30 AMP).

Both Kelsi and I continued to see layers of rebellion peel away inside of us. In prayer, we recognized that we often exerted our wills above God's. The good news was we could and did repent. God is so kind and good.

---

[8]   https://languages.oup.com/google-dictionary-en/

"Know that I am with you always," God said. Great peace accompanied His words.

Another time, these words came loudly into my spirit: "Kathi, I love you!" At those times, I realized just how badly I needed to hear that.

It was so awful to watch Kelsi hit herself. I wanted to jump on her and hold her hands down, but it happened so quickly.

"Get off her now in Jesus's name!" I yelled one day as her hands moved quickly to her forehead.

"Some kind of Mom you are," were the words that came from her. The source was demonic. I felt the anointing of God rise up, and Kelsi was soon relaxed. She hugged me and said it was a spirit of accusation related to the OCD which usually attacked her but this time spewed at me.

"God, I thought things were bad when she was little. I am so tired and worn-out! I don't see how I can keep doing this. What am I not understanding? I know You don't want her doing this," I said. My thoughts continued to spiral downward, and one negative thought piled on top of another. The Holy Spirit interrupted me.

"What're you doing?" He asked. His tone was very friendly. It stopped the cascade.

I praised Him for His constant help. My heart grew steadfast and more confident in faith in Him. As I gave thanks, my faith increased.

When spitting accompanied the frenzied cleaning attempts, I would become angry. The anger exhausted me. I realized that anger promises something it can never deliver. To give vent to unrighteous anger changes nothing. It promises control but really only feeds the evil around it. I repented of this anger because when vented in any way, it was sin.

"You want the hand of God to put things in order," I heard.

I heartily agreed. Kelsi and I both felt very bruised in our spirits.

"Though you have been bruised and beaten, I can cause all of that to be healed in a moment," God spoke.

In spite of the ceaseless pressure, I also felt grateful to God for being alive. It was a shift in my spirit which was another healing.

I realized that God's kingdom operates through our obedience, faith, and giving. It will cost us our pride, dignity, and thought patterns. It may even cost loss of close relationship. I can attest that what we lose is nothing next to what we gain. God knows everything about us because He created us. He knows what He wants to give us.

"Your eyes saw my unformed substance, and in Your book all the days (of my life) were written before ever they took shape, when as yet there was none of them" (Psalm 139:16 AMP). This tells us God knows our purpose and created us with that in mind.

We left the psychiatrist's office after an appointment. As we buckled in, Kelsi handed me her hand sanitizer.

"Use this on the wheel, Mom," she demanded.

Why did I fight it? I usually acquiesced to all her demands but resisted the force of control coming toward me that day.

"No, I don't need to do that," I insisted.

"Mom, you have to use it! It's gross if you don't," she counter-insisted.

"No, I do not need to do that and I'm not going to," I reiterated.

Kelsi got so loud in the car, so angry, and I still didn't cave in that day. I can tell you it wasn't worth it. When we got home, we apologized to each other. When I recall these tough memories, I am so grateful how God always brought us to peace, no matter how loud either of us got with the other.

I heard another prophetic word from Chuck Pierce. I share these because as you read them, you may receive them in faith for yourself! This word was about God taking care of old traumas. "He is realigning your memories from heaven, not from old traumas, so you will be filled with faith no matter how bad situations were that you endured. Faith is invading your memories!"

Both Kelsi and I received this word. Another leader under Chuck Pierce, Marty Cassidy, reported that she experienced two trauma flashbacks but had no recall of the actual events. She felt power and total deliverance from the impact as she was driving her car. This was amazing to hear as it takes a great deal of human effort to heal past traumas. God is present in our yesterdays, our todays, and our futures all at the same time.

"You hem me in, behind and before, and lay your hand upon me" (Psalm 139:5 ESV).

God protects us from the pain of our past, stays present in our now, and is also ahead of us in the future of our time lines. I had seen enough of God healing Kelsi in the present from various past traumas to say yes and amen to that.

# CHAPTER 3

# From Darkness to Light

What doesn't kill you makes you stronger.

—Friedrich Nietzsche

I remember the day Kelsi came home from her day program and went directly up to her room. As I went by her door, she called out to me. I went inside. She was lying down on her bed.

"Mom, today, all of a sudden, I felt real woozy after I worked out and—" She suddenly lost consciousness and stopped speaking.

"Kelsi, wake up! What's the matter?" I demanded as I moved toward her face to see if she was breathing.

Suddenly, she came to again. "I just passed out," she finished the sentence as though she had not done exactly that.

I knew it was from the hitting, and she now had a mild concussion. I ordered a soft kickboxing helmet online so that she would have some protection. I took her to an urgent care place because her family doctor could not see her that day.

She was very tired on the way up and rested. Once we got inside the room with the physician assistant, it was another story.

As she finished her assessment, demons began to manifest with great strength. Kelsi's eyes narrowed, and she shook like an erupting volcano. She sputtered, pursed her lips, and hissed in my direction.

The young professional kept her eyes glued to mine. I realized she did not want to see what was happening.

"Just keep an eye on her, and if she shows any more symptoms, bring her back," she finished.

"Okay, thank you for your time," I said. I held my hand out toward Kelsi, holding ground in the Spirit until we were alone in the room. I steered her out to our car. It felt surreal. Unfortunately, it was not.

I knew the unseen realm just wanted to kick up a demonstration and cause more shame. I refused it. I prayed. Kelsi heard me and came back to herself. We drove home, and she took a nap. She was drained. I remained on high alert.

I so wish I could have made all the attacks cease and desist. No matter how much I prayed or who I took her to see, these attacks continued to erupt. God enabled me to stand with her in all of it.

I cancelled her day program until we got the kickboxing helmet. The team worked on how to curb these behaviors. Her psychiatrist worked on slowing down the motor response. Nothing changed for quite some time. At first, Kelsi was grateful for the helmet, but she came to hate it.

Another problem was that Kelsi dissociated. Sometimes she spoke as a very young child, calling me Mommy, and this was not normal. I explained what was happening to her team.

Dissociation is a mental process of disconnecting from one's thoughts, feelings, memories, or sense of identity. It is a way to cope by avoiding negative emotions related to memories of traumatic events. Highway hypnosis is a mild form of dissociating. You travel a well-known road and do not pay extreme focus to the surroundings. If a deer jumped out, you would notice and slam on the brakes. People dissociate in everyday life. It is a natural response to trauma and can be experienced in many different ways. One could feel the world around them is unreal or that they are viewing themselves from outside their being. One could feel an identity shift and change as in speaking in a younger voice. When it interferes with everyday life, one needs to seek help.

I see dissociation as an effective tool which was designed by God so that children could live through past traumas. When that child grows up, memories may return at any age. In therapy, the adult may then process what they could not before.

For example, if a child is being sexually abused by a father at night, that child must deal with him in the morning. It requires the child to use denial and act as if nothing heinous happened. As an adult, away from the father, parts may safely come forward to tell their stories. In the best cases, integration ensues.

I discussed ways to help Kelsi if she dissociated with her team members. Grounding techniques were often helpful. These could be things like calling out her name, snapping of fingers to get her attention, having her explain her current surroundings, the use of calming smells, etc.

One day in prayer, Kelsi recalled hating herself at age thirteen. She disliked the way she looked and was two years behind her peers in school. She did not feel good about her teachers, and the whole year felt like a "black line." When we prayed, she saw a bunch of different colored strings going out from a center circle. She asked Jesus which line to choose, and He showed her a yellow one. She felt Jesus pull out a deep root that took a while. She felt much relief and gratitude to Jesus who told her she could not do all her healing at once. It would be too much for her to handle. She believed Him.

Some days, I just cried very hard for a while. The Lord stayed with me through everything. As I drew nearer to Him, I felt His emotions. When the court system in New York City legalized late-term abortion, I felt the anger and pain of God. How dare man decide to end life that God brought into being! I prayed and worshipped.

In February, Kelsi had bad nightmares, and the day following was extremely difficult. Spitting and hitting became the norm rather than the exception. This could go on in extreme phases, then it would abate. I found myself yelling out to the Lord in my head as I hugged her. What was the cause of all this torment?

"Like the sparrow in her wandering, like the swallow in her flying, so the causeless curse does not alight" (Proverbs 26:2 AMP).

No curse may alight unless there is a cause. Often, such a cause is due to sin or iniquity in the bloodline. These patterns continue down through the generations until a person with the same DNA repents. I read through Derek Prince's book, *Blessing or Curse, You Can Choose*, and asked God to reveal anything further in His timing.

This understanding came to me after a time of worship. The worst thing generational curses do to us is they prevent us from falling radically in love with Jesus.

Was there still a cause? We had already repented for so many things as God revealed them. Kelsi continued to hit herself on various places in her body. Sometimes she hit her throat or her head. It was a good day if I could redirect her to hit her legs instead.

Kelsi was surprised one time when God showed her many loving memories with me when she was very little. It was hard for her to recall anything positive once the supernatural attacks came, starting at age five.

Kelsi grasped the concept of dissociation immediately. She easily connected with her parts and their various ages. "We're all right here, Mom," she would say. She thought everything was due to her childhood pain, but God explained to her that she had more fear of trusting anyone since she left her job. She thought her boss did her wrong in many ways. When she heard this, she said, "I will never forgive or forget what she did." This is called a vow. In that moment, she almost spat in my face.

"Do not manifest," I said to the demon behind it.

Her face greatly contorted, but my authority held firm. She became peaceful. In prayer, she repented for the vow of unforgiveness, and we broke it. She stated she felt different in a good way.

I'm sure many people believe this is "just" mental illness. They would not pay any attention to the unseen realm. That is a grave mistake. For those who have a hard time believing that spirits operate in another dimension, I refer you to Phil Mason's book, *Quantum Glory: The Science of Heaven Invading Earth*, available on Amazon. When you begin to understand how God created everything from nothing and how science has proven the quirkiness of the quantum realm, your perspective will change. His book totally upholds what we read in the Bible. Jesus cast out demons all the time.

John and I began praying Psalm 91 over our family. I began writing some articles for GOD TV online. The Lord told me to give him all the pain.

One especially hard day, Kelsi cried out to God to help her. She said Jesus chose a light-blue string to follow to a memory. When she saw a tunnel, she got nervous and came to ask me to pray with her. As I stayed in prayer, she explained what happened this time.

"This looked like a long journey, so I asked Jesus what the point of the string was. Could it be cut? Jesus said not until I knew what it was. I got to a place where I danced with Jesus, and it felt wonderful. Then I got to an emotion of when I was seven years old. I was really disturbed!" This was the first time I saw her recognize this truth. With the help of Jesus in the memory, she was able to see the demonic oppression without being in it. Some of the worst manifestations happened that year.

I reminded her this was not her fault, and I was sorry for putting any of my emotions on her at that time. She asked to be alone with the Lord, so I left the room. Later, she told me she held herself at age seven as Jesus had His arms around them both. She said Jesus said it was time to cut the cord. He touched it. It became ashes. Kelsi experienced integration as she said "she became one with me." That part never resurfaced after that day.

This is exactly what we want to see to heal fragmentation. It's just that Jesus did it alone for her without me even needing to be in the room.

She then explained when she received healing in these layers, it affects the rest of the colored lines. It makes a difference for all of them. She understood integration because she experienced it. This was because Jesus accepted all parts of her, attuned to her emotions, and led her to peace.

One time, Kelsi said she chose to follow a pink string, and she came to a heavenly mansion. She decided to "let my imagination run wild," and she went shopping for different halos. She was not experiencing any trauma with this, and I did not feel from the Lord to ask about it. It was good to see her have fun.

Kelsi saw a DVD story about Ananias and Sapphira in the book of Acts. They were a husband and wife who agreed to lie to the Apostle Peter about the price of land they had sold. Because of this, they both died in front of Peter. Kelsi became very angry at God. I tried to reason with her, but it had no impact.

Then God firmly answered her, "Kelsi, stop it! This was my church! I am holy, and that holiness had to be respected!"

Immediately, Kelsi calmed down. Now I could explain that His entire church would have been infected by the lying. They were all very closely knit together at that time. Peter knew they lied because he was full of the Holy Spirit.

Would we be ready for such a manifestation of the Holy Spirit in our churches or homes? It certainly brought forth the awe of God. I believe a spirit of true worship is coming because God told me He is "changing the atmosphere."

I heard Kelsi loudly defending me one day. She said the demons were saying very bad things about me. She replied, "I say she's a great person! Now go away!" The interesting thing was I was feeling depressed for a while before I heard the ruckus. It lifted after Kelsi got rid of them.

Kelsi saw a red string in prayer which took her back to my maternal grandmother. I had never been close to her as a child. As He often did, Jesus worked on me at the same time He helped Kelsi. I forgave my grandmother, and both Kelsi and I felt a deep release with ensuing peace. She also said Jesus cut the cord between her and me so Kelsi would begin to truly grow up emotionally. She would often feel relief after our prayer times. True healing came in layers, yet the evil onslaught continued.

Then Kelsi had an encounter in the courts of heaven.

This day, Jesus put His hand on Kelsi's back and took her to His court. He said, "It's okay, you are not in trouble. This is a different kind of court." Then Jesus asked Kelsi's spirit to take control of her brain. Kelsi trusted Jesus very much. It was easy for Him to enable her to ascend in her spirit to be in that realm.

Kelsi noticed that when she was there with Jesus, she didn't have any problems at all. She felt more at ease than when she was here in the flesh. "I need help. It's not easy. I can't control my brain," she told me. Here is what she saw when she ascended.

"Whoa, Mom, it looks like a courtroom! I am sitting in a side box. Someone is reading a scroll about some gross things I did in the past. They are accusing me of hurting myself constantly. Now they closed the scroll. Mom, Jesus says it would be good for you as my mom to repent for any sins you committed against me as a child that made me believe lies about myself."

I immediately repented for everything I could think of. More evil spirits came forth.

Jesus asked, "What is your complaint against my daughter?"

Kelsi heard the following.

"She is an absolute fool. She doesn't deserve to go on living. Look at her, she may be fine in spirit, but when she goes back into her flesh, she is a pathetic meat sack. She is the queen of refuse."

"What is refuse, Mom?" Kelsi asked.

"It's like garbage, honey," I said. My faith soared again as I knew she was not making this up.

She then heard more demonic voices say, "Bow down to her, queen of slut, putrid, refuse, smelly muck." Kelsi never spoke like this. The fact that she did not know the word *refuse* was also more evidence that she was hearing from the unseen realm.

Kelsi then repented for believing she was any of those things. "That is not who I am. I am a child of God created by Him!"

She heard Jesus say, "Enough said. Now leave," and everything scattered away. Jesus then asked, "Does anyone else have a problem with Kelsi?"

She stated, "Mom, He is my Papa God, my lion!" After such encounters, she slept. She awoke with more clarity.

I found confirmation about this healing session through Robert Henderson's book, *Operating in the Courts of Heaven*. Mr. Henderson states that we need to know the language of the courts in heaven. The Bible describes an amazing scene.

> As I looked, thrones were placed, and the
> Ancient of Days took his seat; his clothing was

white as snow, and the hair of his head like pure wool; his throne was fiery flames; its wheels were burning fire. A stream of fire issued and came out from before him; a thousand thousands served him, and ten thousand times ten thousand stood before him; the court sat in judgment, and the books were opened. (Daniel 7:9, 10 ESV)

We see that the court is seated in heaven. Then the books are opened. I assumed Jesus had already taken care of all of this since He told Kelsi He wanted to take her up there.

Mr. Henderson explains about the counsel of the Lord and the books of heaven through the scriptures.

For those whom He foreknew, He also predestined to be conformed to the image of His Son, that He might be the firstborn among many brothers. And those whom He predestined, He also called, and those whom He called He also justified, and those whom He justified, He also glorified. (Romans 8:29–30 ESV)

In other words, Mr. Henderson explains that God foreknew us.

Before we existed, there was a book written about us in heaven from the counsel of the Lord. We are predestined which means God sent us into earth with a plan. We can discover it or disregard what is in our book. If we do find our purpose God gives us His Grace to fulfill our purpose. We are called by God so what He has written in our book is written on our heart. Holy Spirit must unveil this to us. We are justified which means we are rendered just or innocent so that no accusations can stick to us. This is critical to understand as a follower of Jesus. The

Accuser, Satan, presents evidence to God, who is the Judge, about why He cannot legally grant to us what is written in our book. We must answer these accusations by the Blood of Jesus and with necessary repentance. Then God as Judge of all can fulfill His passion toward us and grant us what is in our book. We are glorified when we fully step into what is written in our book. Our judgment is based on how closely we live our lives with what is written in our heavenly book. Our job is to discover and fulfill what is in our book and bring it to earth.[9]

Cases can be presented in court when the books are opened. Dominion rights of evil powers can be removed from us.

This made sense to me. Earth is a shadow or copy of heaven. We have courts here on the earth of various types and with different degrees of authority. Courts exist in heaven. As we grow in holiness before the Lord, we gain authority in those courts. Heaven recognizes that we are walking in a manner worthy of Jesus. It is God's grace that empowers us to live above sin.

I highly recommend Mr. Henderson's book. As I said, it was a helpful resource during this time of prayer.

In March of 2019, just before our battle intensified, God connected very strongly with me. In a dream, He left me a beautiful note written in gold with these words: "I just want you to know how much I love you." That dream strengthened me for what lay ahead.

Her psychiatrist started Latuda, an atypical antipsychotic medication, because he said she had excess dopamine in her brain and he needed to slow down her motor response. Over the next five months, we tried different amounts because of side effects. As we went up on the Latuda, she complained she felt "too loose and emotional." She

---

[9] *The Books of Heaven. Operating in the Courts of Heaven: Granting God the Legal Rights to Fulfill His Passion and... Answer Our Prayers* (Robert Henderson Ministries, 2016) pp.35–40.

also experienced tremors. Then we started propranolol to deal with the tremors. We started progesterone drops to help her hormonal imbalances. By August, she was scratching deep marks in her desk in an effort to not hit herself, and we increased her daily dose of Celexa.

In the midst of this, we continued to have prayer sessions. Jesus told me to repent for generational hardheartedness, and as I did so, I felt a deep release inside. I resolved to fight for Kelsi from a place of rest in Jesus rather than in my own strength.

I do not want to glorify the difficulties of our battle. I also do not want to avoid them. To be totally honest, this part of Kelsi's life was horrendous. God truly strengthened me to write the first four chapters of this book.

One morning, Kelsi burst into my room at 5:00 a.m., hit her head, and returned to her room. I hung my head.

"God, I don't know what to do anymore," I said.

"You've done it before," He said.

"What? What do you mean, God?" I asked.

"Restore order," He said.

That night, I prayed a massive deliverance prayer, taking the strongest stance against the enemy that I had yet attempted.

Kelsi shook and cried. She hugged me. "Wow, Mom, what a relief!" she exclaimed. At the same time, she said it would take more time and prayer for fuller healing.

We saw a spirit-filled psychologist who prayed for Kelsi several times. She always felt much better after he laid hands on her. When we came back from one session, she said a younger part of her wanted to tell me something but only in writing. Later, she left a small pink sticky note in my prayer room with the words "I adore you, Mommy" written on it. It surprised me, but I knew this was the expression of a younger part of her emotional makeup. I accepted her gift with joy. There was no integration this time, but it was very healing for both of us.

We moved into April. It was a crazy time. There were the team meetings, new personnel coming onboard, behavior specialists to handle the hitting and medication appointments, and changes that didn't really work. Initially, Kelsi was grateful for the helmet, but over time, I had to enforce her keeping it on. The motor response came on too fast. That was the absolute hardest part, watching her swiftly and repeatedly hitting herself.

"John, I am so overwhelmed and agitated watching this. It is horrendous, and I feel so helpless. I don't know how much longer Kelsi or I can do this," I said through my tears.

"Kathi, you just bulldoze your way through things," he said.

The phone rang, and I had to answer it. Later, I wondered, was it a good thing to be a bulldozer? I prayed about it. Then I thought of what a bulldozer does. They are powerful machines that break up ground. They move, destroy, or knock down or create something like a road. To bulldoze can also mean to force something to be done in a harsh way. I repented for any defiled bulldozing I had done in life. I asked Jesus to create godly bulldozing in my life, for Kelsi's freedom, and for our family. It was the next day before I asked my husband to clarify his statement.

"I mean you get it done! It's a good thing," he reassured me.

I was struck by how much I tended to lean toward the negative in any type of self-appraisal.

When God pointed out a need for repentance, I obeyed. I heard Him say, "I was wrong" but did not know what it meant until I prayed with Kelsi again. Suddenly, I told her I was wrong in some of my negative beliefs about her as a child. I found myself feeling so hopeless at times. Unfortunately, as happens with all of us, she took my beliefs in. After she received my apology, she realized that she was wrong when she hit herself as a form of self-punishment. It didn't stop the hitting at this point, but the insight surfaced.

Kelsi had much sleep disruption. In the middle of the night, I heard her agitated movements in her bedroom. I opened her door and just sat on her bed and prayed.

"Why are you staying in here, Mom? Don't you need sleep?" Kelsi asked.

"Because you need help, and I'm your Mom," I said.

She relaxed and fell asleep. The next morning, she said, "I feel more normal today." Three things contributed to her brief improvement. I repented for my past sins. She saw the sin of self-abuse. In love and compassion, I sacrificed sleep to help her.

I was almost asleep one night when the Holy Spirit stated, "He was murdered."

I knew He referred to what happened to Jesus. He was outrageously and deliberately killed. Mankind did it unlawfully and with malice. It means there was great desire to cause Him pain with intent to commit such a heinous act without any legal justification or excuse. I had not thought this deeply about it. It made me more aware of the depth of all the sin of mankind, including my own. It emphasized how much Jesus was hated by evil spirits that worked through men in this way. I knew evil spirits hated us. Kelsi and I had been on the end of that punching bag for years. But when God spoke those three words to me, the depth of the hatred reverberated through my being.

> If the world hates you, know that it has hated me before it hated you. If you were of the world, the world would love you as its own; but because you are not of the world, but I chose you out of the world, therefore the world hates you. (John 15:18, 19 ESV)

"[T]hey hated me without a cause" (John 15: 25 ESV).

Another day, Kelsi heard God say He wanted her to come to Him instead of hitting herself. "He said something about heavy lade? What is that word, Mom?" she asked.

I told her God knew she was "heavy-laden," and He wanted her to experience His rest.

She saw herself walk upstairs into some clouds, and she hugged God. "It's a good thing He's doing for me," she said.

In the midst of all the trauma, drama, and prayers, we used the Word of God by faith. Kelsi recognized that so many of her thoughts were not her own. They were from the enemy. She did her best to extinguish them, yet they were relentless, no matter what medications we tried. When she made bad choices in movies or TV shows, there were consequences to pay because these ignited more of her ungodly imagination. I would bless her spirit to receive the goodness of God and focus on righteous choices.

> Consider it a sheer gift, friends, when tests and challenges come at you from all sides. You know that under pressure, your faith-life is forced into the open and shows its true colors. So don't try to get out of anything prematurely. Let it do its work so you become mature and well-developed, not deficient in any way. If you don't know what you're doing, pray to the Father. He loves to help. (James 1:3–5, The Message)

While I cannot say I saw our trials as a "sheer gift" when they were happening, I did recognize how our faith was developing through them. We did not hesitate to pray frequently due to our intense need for God. We remained committed to seeking Him. We kept our focus on Him. We saw Him who is invisible on a daily basis by faith. We did not give up. We kept our eyes on the prize because we knew that faith was an ongoing fight. We cannot escape the fight and still keep our faith. We fight so we may finish our race. The Apostle Paul put it this way: "I have fought the good fight, I have finished the race, I have kept the faith" (2 Timothy 4:7 ESV).

God told me to read Isaiah 14. I pondered this chapter which is about the Lord who has compassion on us and gives relief from suffering, turmoil, and cruel bondage. He notes that the oppressor has come to an end, and He has broken the rod of the wicked. I knew that God was preparing to make it easier for us on the road ahead. I just didn't know what was on that road. I prayed to be as obedient as Esther in the Bible. She submitted to a pagan king and rose above it all as her kingdom assignment.

God spoke and gently reminded me, "I am inside you." This restored my hope again.

My pastor's wife asked me to speak at a conference in the fall. I asked God what to convey.

"Teach them there is hope for the hopeless, rest in the midst of tremendous pressure, and peace in any storm," He instructed.

I knew I was living this through His power.

God asked me to attend a "Summer of Glory" conference hosted by David Herzog ministries in Phoenix, Arizona, in June of 2019. How did I know He wanted me to go? When I saw the e-mail with the invitation, I felt a huge surge of joy inside my being, though my soul did not understand it. I ignored it for a week or two. I felt too tired and did not want to leave Kelsi with all her struggles. However, I felt compelled to return and search for that e-mail because I knew that emotional experience was supernatural, and God does things for His own reasons. I made all the necessary changes to my schedule.

After this, I heard God say I have "friends in court." Psalm 94:15 tells us that "judgment will again be founded on righteousness and all the upright in heart will follow it." We all need friends in heaven's courtrooms!

Kelsi's spiritual counselor laid hands on her. He reassured her that the Lord said nothing was her fault for all the trauma. He said that truth needed to get down deep inside of her. Kelsi continued to wake up a lot at night, and I kept praying for her recovery. On May 19, Kelsi turned twenty-nine years old. We celebrated her birthday with her small group of friends. They met at a local restaurant. I was so grateful for the three friends she had—Kayla, Patrick, and Susan.

Two days later, Kelsi ferociously hit the top of her head. God came through me in total love.

"Stop," I said with compassion. I reached out and hugged her without any anxiety or frustration. She calmed down in response to God's voice coming through me. We talked about hating what God hates. He hates mental illness. Kelsi didn't know that God hated anything, but He hates evil.

It was our forty-third wedding anniversary, and I woke at 3:00 a.m. to hear Kelsi banging on the floor in the bathroom. She was hitting herself and spitting on the floor as compulsive behaviors to counteract strong emotions attached to her thoughts. I began to pray in desperation to not lose my mind, to stay steady with her through this. God reminded me of my reading from the previous day. "They who sow in tears shall reap in joy and singing. He who goes forth bearing seed and weeping shall doubtless come again with rejoicing, bringing his sheaves with him" (Psalm 126:5, 6 AMP). This held me until Kelsi could stop the behavior and pray.

"I feel huge hate. It's a red string. Mom, I can't be healed," she said in despair.

I cried out to God, and Kelsi felt His touch. God showed us the power of "idle words" spoken in our generational line, and we repented for those careless things we and our ancestors had spoken over others. She cried and rested again. She felt too emotional on the Latuda, so her psychiatrist decreased the dosage. We went up and down on the dosage over the next five months. We also tried breaking up the dosages throughout the day. She complained of tremors from Latuda, and the hitting did not stop. We increased propranolol. We tried everything the psychiatrist suggested. It just didn't help. I never saw anyone try as hard as Kelsi did. Her life was heroic.

As I rested one day, I saw a faint image that looked like an angel. A knowing suddenly came to me that God was giving me a new grace, something I did not have before. Within a few days, God showed me that the new grace was to see the power of community. I looked upon the earth in the spirit and saw many people who were "lit up" for Jesus. Kelsi told me she took "spiritual communion," which was to take the bread and cup in the spirit, not the natural. I began to incorporate this into my life.

Kelsi had a dream where she heard, "Come let us adore Him." It impacted her greatly. When she had a session with our friend, Denise, she agreed to start goals for her thoughts. When she would have a "bad" thought about herself, she agreed to look into a mirror and say out loud, "I don't deserve that." Kelsi felt the weight of holiness on this and cried in relief back home.

God is ever-present and lovingly willing to help us in all things large and small. When the fumes from the self-cleaning function on our oven gave me a headache, I asked God to remove it. The smell was gone instantly, though the oven continued to run for three hours. Most importantly, Kelsi continued to be tormented, yet He always showed up to ease things. He did not heal her here. He spoke to my husband about that initially after she moved to heaven, and later, He spoke to me and showed me more about it.

At one of her team meetings, the behavior specialist said there had been a "20 percent reduction in hitting."

The next day, Kelsi yelled out loud, "I am sick of this hitting!"

That was a good sign. Now her will was engaged to fight it. It was also at this time that I found out about electric bikes from some friends who did not know Jesus. I thought to get one for myself because it would be easier to drive than my much heavier scooter. I also felt God's love for these friends and prayed for them to come to know Him.

Kelsi had been riding her regular bike for many years all around town. She walked to the library safely. That was the extent of her freedom. When we decided to get an electric bike, it was mainly for me. My scooter was too heavy for me, and I wanted something lighter. We have a long driveway with a steep incline. An e-bike would facilitate our ability to traverse the final lap to our garage.

I knew Kelsi would truly enjoy the ease of this bike. There was so little joy in her life. She had gradually been improving in focus, attention, and mood as noted by her staff people. I taught her how to ride it. We went over all the rules every day for safe handling. I followed closely behind her on my scooter or in my car to observe her reactions. She was only allowed to drive on a few specific back roads around our small town.

Previous to this time, Kelsi had been evaluated to see if she could learn to drive a car. She knew the rules in the book better than I did. I remember when she warned me about an obscure rule as we drove on the highway. That evaluator felt she could learn to drive, but we felt that was not possible. She was disappointed. Her two best friends had autism but were able to drive a car. She was grateful for the new freedom with the e-bike.

I specifically told her not to go on the road where she was hit by a car. I do not know if she thought about the danger that day. I do know that a friend saw her about fifteen minutes before the accident at another intersection. I had told her to turn back at the stop sign there because the road became narrow and windy, and traffic could increase. I was comforted when my friend told me how she stopped, nodded, turned the bike around, and headed back toward home as I had instructed her to do. Instead of returning home, she continued on the back road to the intersection where she was hit.

Kelsi told me, "You don't know how hard it is for me to be here some days, Mom." Soon after that, she prayed and said God told her there is hope for all the hell she was going through. God said He hated what she was enduring. He said He cared about her, and she felt caring hands on her arms. He said the torment was going to stop.

"It makes me know I have a God who is here! I am cared for and I matter. I am one of zillions of people, but I felt nobody cared for me, especially in high school," she said. Her countenance always changed to peace when she heard God. It never occurred to me how the torment was going to stop in her life. I assumed it meant she would be healed of mental illness while she was still here. In fact, I always expected that. I knew others around me did not, but somehow, I did.

I read a teaching by Rick Joyner which quoted 2 Corinthians 3:18. "We all with unveiled face beholding as in a mirror the glory of the Lord are being transformed into the same image from glory to glory." We need to seek His glory so we may be changed. We cannot first change enough so that we may be good enough to see His glory. Just seek Him.

I felt that I was to write and teach a six-part Bible study about joy. I obeyed and taught two of the lessons in the late summer of 2019.

Kelsi and I had three great trips in August. We went to Hersheypark Gardens and Museum. We went to the shore together and parasailed again. This time, Kelsi totally enjoyed herself, and I got many great pictures of us being up in the air. We also went with her dance academy to see the play *Frozen* in New York City. She was relaxed and much better during these trips. We both believed in hope that the worst was over.

The next day, I flew to Phoenix for the conference as God instructed me to do. The first night I was there, I was awakened by a heavenly voice.

"Just so you know, those mental health problems will be gone before your next birthday. You will fill up three times with Father, Son, and Holy Spirit."

I was immediately enraptured and enthralled about what I heard! God was going to heal Kelsi before October 29! That was only a month away!

I met a new friend at the conference who was on a twenty-one-day fast. She asked God for a word for me. The day after I heard that mental illness would end, she told me what she heard.

"Kathi, these problems with your daughter are not supposed to keep going on and on. I heard it will be done by the end of the year," she said.

Again, I received this as a confirming word because I expected Kelsi to be healed here in the earth realm. My new friend had lost her adult son a few years earlier from an unexpected brain bleed. I did not perceive the connecting thread.

There were a number of supernatural healings at this conference. Metal dissolved out of bodies. The speakers were on fire for God. I made a new friend who would be a great comfort in the trial ahead.

God doesn't think like we do. The Bible assures us of that truth.

"For My thoughts are not your thoughts, neither are your ways My ways, says the Lord. For as the heavens are higher than the earth, so are My ways higher than your ways and My thoughts than your thoughts" (Isaiah 55:8, 9 AMP).

I know this to be so. I have learned it very deeply through the single biggest heartbreak of my life. My daughter, Kelsi, moved to heaven on September 27, 2019, after being hit by a car. Her body died, but her spirit simply kicked off that shell and went home to be with Jesus. She was totally healed. No more torment would be able to assail her mind. Her healing did not happen here. It happened there when she went home.

# CHAPTER 4

# The Day Kelsi Moved Home

I'll see you soon, Mom.

—Kelsi Basehore

G od spoke very clearly and directly to me in the midst of unimaginable pain. Over 80 percent of the sympathy cards we received said "For some things, there are just no words." People cared and were horrified. I am sure some imagined how devastated they would feel if it happened in their family. For those who had lost children of their own, empathy and understanding came forth as they shared their stories of loss and eventual stabilization into their new normal.

John and I left for the day to get a used car in Maryland. Kelsi had plans for the morning with her autism support person. Her behavior specialist recently told me they were now seeing "great improvement." As Kelsi went to the door, she turned around for our goodbye ritual. She had started this as a very young child. "Rub cheeks, Mom," she used to say. She found it very comforting to rub one cheek, then the other, against mine. "Yours are so soft," she would say. This gave her strength to start her day. That is the last time I saw her alive. She came home after lunch. She took out my electric bike and had the accident.

For most of her life, I had Kelsi on a very short leash. I was constantly with her, following or observing her when we went places.

She always meant to be responsible but would forget to turn her cell phone volume up. When I allowed her to walk in the mall alone, I would call, and she would not answer. Then with anxiety, I would search for her. I remember one time I had walked the entire mall and came to the last store which had an escalator. I asked a man where to go to report someone missing. He told me to go upstairs. I prayed, "God, You know where she is. Please lead me."

As I rounded the corner to ascend on the moving platform, there she was, a few steps ahead. She turned and smiled.

"Oh, hi, Mom," she said.

I sighed with relief. After that, I always checked to make sure the volume was up on her phone, and we tested before we parted. She often met her friends at the mall, and they behaved very responsibly together.

Kelsi hated being on the leash, whether it was with me or her autism waiver staff. The lack of freedom caused much anger at times. She felt trapped. As she hit her mid-twenties, she got disgusted with herself for still living at home. This went on for several months until God gave me the words to say.

"Kelsi, you won't be here forever. Neither will I. Why don't you just enjoy your home and relax outside at the pool as long as you are here? I know things will change for you in the future," I said.

She brightened up and was not bothered about it anymore.

This fateful day, John and I were driving home from Maryland when I saw a text from my sister, Jan. She asked if we could "pull over," but it was not possible as we were flowing in traffic. I sensed something was very wrong, so I told her to call me. When she did, she again asked if we could stop the car. Now I felt dread.

"Just tell me, Jan," I said. My mouth went dry, and all the muscles in my body tightened.

"Kelsi was in an accident. She was hit by a car," she blurted out.

"No, no, oh my God, no," was all I could say.

"She didn't make it!" Jan cried.

"*Oh my God, oh my God, oh my God!*" I repeated over and over, stunned, in shock. "*No, no, no, no, no!*"

"What's the matter?" John demanded. He looked at me, then quickly put his eyes back on the road.

"Kelsi was hit, and she died," I sputtered out with my head down in agony and shock.

"*What?*" John yelled while keeping his eyes on the road.

We made it to the hospital because angels were ministering to both of us in the car. Jan told me our sister, Jill, and her husband, Rob, were already at the hospital but could not see her until we got there. I called the hospital. I called Jill. I said we were coming. Oh my God, we wouldn't get there for another two hours! I could not take it in.

Finally, we pulled into the parking lot at the emergency room. I showed John where to park, and we walked in together.

There was a mass of humanity in the waiting room. I could see people suffering with mental health issues walking about, muttering to themselves, gesturing with their arms. Others sat silently, waiting for someone to help them. I gave our names, and they walked us back to the room where Jill and Rob were waiting. The coroner's assistant came in and talked. She told us details—too many details. It took too long. It was amazing to me how polite I was. I wanted to scream at her, "Lady, we just lost our daughter! Enough! Let us see her!"

I cut through the monologue. "May we please see her now," I said.

We began to follow them through the hallways. As we came through the last door, I saw her. She was fully exposed because the door to her room was open. The hospital apologized to me later when I told them that. *No, no, no, no, no.* We walked toward her room, and I wanted to throw up.

"We will go in alone," I told them.

They closed the door behind us, and John wept for our daughter. I could not cry. I touched her repeatedly, stroked her face, kissed her cheek, and told her I loved her. John kissed her and touched her foot. I felt the bulge at her abdomen under the covers, so I knew she had internal damage. Oh, the horror. The devastation. The shock.

Some time passed. I allowed Jill and Rob to see her to say their goodbyes. The chaplain came in, held our hands, and prayed with us.

I looked at the chair next to her bed. There were her few belongings. These included her helmet, shoes, and I think a sock was in the bag. We had to go. I knew she was not there any longer. Her skin was still soft as I pressed my cheek to hers.

"Goodbye, Bubba," I mumbled. "I don't want to leave her," I pleaded with the chaplain even as we walked away. It felt so impossible to simply go home without her. She had been with us for twenty-nine years! Every room in our house was full of her presence. Now our home would be so horribly empty.

I got a call around 10:00 p.m., asking about organ donation since Kelsi had listed herself as a donor. I got through that call on automatic pilot too.

Finally, I fell into bed, screaming inside my head, *Please let me see her, God!*

I heard the words, "Kelsi would like to talk to you," but I could not assimilate this. Suddenly, I heard "This is not the Holy Spirit. This is Mercy." I came to understand it was the very intervention of the Lord Jesus Himself. A warm blanket covered my entire body from the unseen realm. In a state of immediate relaxation, I slept. In the morning, I lay listless in my bed. The sun was ridiculously bright outside my window. What reason did I have to get up? To live?

Suddenly, this thought came. The only difference between myself and my daughter now was that Kelsi's spirit was out of her body and in heaven. My spirit was still encased in my body. Immediately, a tiny but very bright white circle of light danced off my windowsill. Out of that light emerged these words, "I'll see you soon, Mom."

A great calm enveloped me. I was in awe that God opened up my eyes to see into the spirit realm in order to receive this amazing communication. Kelsi didn't say goodbye to me. The words God allowed me to see conveyed truth. We would be reunited one day in eternity. This is in accordance with Scripture. In John 14:2, Jesus said, "In My Father's house are many rooms. If it were not so, would I have told you that I go to prepare a place for you?"

I cannot tell you how much seeing those words saved my sanity. Kelsi indeed did want to "talk to me," yet I knew it was only because the Lord allowed it.

The words I saw were further confirmed by Kat Kerr, a spirit-filled woman of God who has been taken by the Spirit of God to heaven on numerous occasions. She is the president of One Quest International. Her URL is https://www.revealingheaven.com/one-quest/.

On one of her podcasts, Kat explains that our loved ones who die before us don't miss us in heaven because they expect us! She says heaven views these things very differently than we do. "When someone dies, we have a funeral here, but they have a party there." The idea of being able to somehow celebrate Kelsi's "graduation" to heaven was so hard for me to comprehend.

Chuck Pierce is an apostolic leader of Glory of Zion church in Corinth, Texas. Their URL is www.gloryofzion.org. On that Sunday following the accident, he prophesied these words: "Some of you have had loved ones die this week that you wish were here today. The beauty of grace is, God brings what's in the ashes into a new form. All those lost battles and those seeds went into the ground. Call forth victory over them and decree you will see them rise in a new way this week."

His words hit me like a shock wave. I never heard him prophesy that before or since. It was a word of the Lord for me and for many other people.

My sister, Jill, reminded me of something I had said after Kelsi received her first diagnosis at age five. It was actually a prophecy, but I did not recognize it at the time.

"Don't you remember? You said that Kelsi would be healed by the time she was thirty years old," Jill said. The memory returned to me. Kelsi was diagnosed at age five with a form of autism. She was age twenty-nine when she moved to heaven. Suddenly, another memory came to me. This was something Kelsi said a few weeks before her accident occurred.

"Mom, I always thought I'd be healed by the time I'm thirty," she said as she ran by me to go outside.

I knew I had never mentioned my prophecy to her because I did not even remember it until Jill retrieved it. It was one of those God moments. Why would she even say that?

Now we had to decide about a funeral. We did not have Kelsi cremated. She told me one time she did not want me to choose that option for myself. I know that choice is fine, but it bothered Kelsi in her humanity to think about it. I wanted to give my family a chance to see her and say their goodbyes. The whole idea of a public funeral put me into a tailspin. I could not do it. The pressure lifted when this thought came to me.

We would have a private funeral for our family. Kelsi would not care. She was with God in joy. More peace enveloped me. Perhaps we could hold a memorial service later. The pain was so great we could hardly get through the days. People could understand or not. It didn't matter.

I could not believe that this was how Kelsi's sufferings came to an end. For years, I had believed that at some point, she would be healed. It would be a great testimony to the power of Jesus. My mind kind of went into a tilt. Why, God? I don't get it! I had faith for this. We went through multiple deliverance sessions. I prayed with her. I laid hands on her and saw layers of healing. I took her to many spirit-filled counselors. We all got baptized as adults. We spoke in tongues. I believed You and Your word. I even cast out demons when they showed up! I stood in faith for this for twenty-four years!

> He who believes (who adheres to and trust in and relies on the Gospel and Him Whom it sets forth) and is baptized will be saved (from the penalty of eternal death); but he who does not believe will be condemned. And these attesting signs will accompany those who believe; in My Name they will drive out demons; they will speak in new languages; they will pick up serpents; and (even) if they drink anything deadly, it will not hurt them; they will lay their hands on the sick, and they will get well. (Mark 16:16–18 AMP)

That was one of my favorite passages in the whole Bible. When others around me were not touting those scriptures, I did.

I felt like the psalmist David when he began to pour out his heart to God. God can handle emotions. I went into a deeper place of lament-laden worship. This included my expression of all shock, confusion, pain, and anger. God met me there. He drew me out when I disengaged from Him in profound overwhelming disappointment and rage. He cannot be other than good. Only now do I truly know this.

"And Jesus said to him, 'Why do you call Me good? No one is good except God alone" (Mark 10:18 ESV).

Kelsi's favorite song was "This Is Me" from the movie *The Greatest Showman.* I used to hear her sing and dance to it with abandon in her room. She didn't care if I watched. In spite of all the enemy did in his attempts to destroy her, she fought back. She sought God. We prayed together. We did not give up. This song still makes me cry.

Kelsi identified with the pain of all the performers in the movie. They felt like outcasts. Yet her resilience shone through the words. She fought back against all the evil that attacked her in her life. She was a warrior.

She actually became who she was created to be when she left this world and entered the celestial one. In that place now with the Lord Jesus Christ, totally healed and loved, she is now without a doubt glorious.

I do believe there was a huge celebration in heaven to welcome her home. I was so thankful God opened my eyes in the spirit realm to see the words from her. I had not asked for anything like that. God, in His extreme grace and mercy, allowed it. Yet the grief was more intense than I can adequately describe. I did not really believe I would come through it to the other side. God had a lot to say to me about all of this. I was very amazed at the understanding I received over the next several months.

CHAPTER 5

# Listening to God Is Lifesaving

Listen to advice and accept instruction, that
you may gain wisdom in the future.

—Proverbs 19:20 ESV

I want to remind the reader that I am simply telling my story. Everyone must grieve in their own way. If you know the Lord Jesus, listening to the voice of Father God will help you more than anything else will. He may not speak to you as He did to me, or in the same timing. He did not speak that way to my friend Denise, who has a deep relationship with God. She told me it took her much longer to wade through her grief regarding her son's passing.

About one week after Kelsi's funeral, I asked God a simple question, and His answer was very direct. "God, how can You possibly expect me to live with all this grief, pain, and guilt?"

"Because I got her," He said immediately. That stopped me. It was in a very conversational tone. He did not sound at all upset. That also greatly surprised me because I was in turmoil. But His Voice, as always, kept me from going over the edge. After hearing Him so clearly, I determined that I would get through this by the power of the spirit of God. By His love and grace, I would run my race with endurance. I certainly recognized I had no might or power here. My beautiful Kelsi moved "TO HEAVEN," God interjected into my thoughts. He was very careful to correct my thoughts when I was about to look at this through my soul. We did not lose her. She simply went ahead of us.

The night after God told me He got her, I woke up very early. As I lay helplessly in bed, I felt debilitating despair and emptiness. Suddenly, I felt something rub my right cheek, and I heard the words "rub cheeks." I was amazed, and tears ran down my face as I lay there in the dark, knowing God had allowed that connection with Kelsi also. I was filled with awe and peace, knowing she was right there. Nobody else knew that was our daily signature connection. I have heard that the veil between heaven and earth is very thin. There have been many reports of people seeing their loved ones right in front of them as they prepare to transition to the next realm. Other prophetic people report that they hear people from the cloud of witnesses cheering them on, especially when they are giving the word of the Lord to others. This sovereignly allowed event cinched it for me.

Then I felt panic because I had not thought to even attempt to raise Kelsi from the dead. (That mandate is also in Mark 16. I have known evangelists who have done this in the power of the Holy Spirit.) I called Denise. She was such a strong support for me the first several months. Her son, Adam, had moved to heaven several years before, and when she and her daughters gathered around him to pray, they all knew he did not want to come back. Denise's answer was simple and comforting.

"The Holy Spirit would have nudged you to do that. If it didn't occur to you, it's because He didn't want it done. He can cut through all of our panic and emotions to get that message through," she said. I came back to sanity again.

Songs often set me into a tailspin of grief. I prayed and asked God to protect me from this onslaught. I avoided listening to any music for quite some time.

The last memories of our three trips haunted me. When we went to Ocean City, New Jersey, we had the most fun of all. As we drove home, I remembered her smiling at me and saying, "This was a good trip, Mom!" We had fun shopping though it poured the day we went to Atlantic City. We ate at the Rainforest Café on the boardwalk there. We played at a different mini-golf place off the boardwalk. We redeemed our parasailing experience from the previous year, when Kelsi had a meltdown before we were hoisted into the air. We did everything she wanted to do. I am so glad for that, yet in these early days, the grief overwhelmed everything.

A few days later, God said, "I am with you." I felt pain surge about Kelsi. He said, "I'm not seeing this as a tragedy." That was the word everyone was using. I agreed. But He did not!

The following Sunday, some people found a church fan that Kelsi had written on. "Leave this fan in it too! Don't touch my Bible, the fan too! Leave it alone! Now! (Me, Kelsi!) Leave this where I left off at! Please!" On Sundays, she would read the church Bible that was stashed in the pew box. She placed the fan directly under the last words she had been reading. She expected to pick it up the next week and resume reading from that point onward. Of course, other people would pull the fan out of the Bible to use it. When Kelsi eventually returned to that exact spot it would no longer be where she had left it. It was a bittersweet Kelsi-wink to see that fan. I kept it.

Denise texted me that God told her to tell me at that very moment, He had my heart in his hands. I just wanted to die and go to heaven to see Kelsi.

Most days I wailed like a crazy person. Right after the accident, I did not eat anything for four or five days. I simply could not do it. When I did eat, it was once a day with very small portions. In the first few months, I lost about twenty pounds. My siblings were very supportive. My youngest sister, Heidi, often visited and brought food.

"She was here, right? She actually existed?" I found myself asking. Looking back, I simply experienced "derealization." This is a dissociative state that comes on during extreme stress. I didn't know what was real. My brain broke and handled the trauma the only way it could. I didn't deny Kelsi was gone. I questioned whether she had ever been here. This state came and went for a while. It lessened as I embraced the truth and emptiness of the new now.

During this time, I learned something more about the power of tongues. I remember screaming and crying upstairs, and I could not get my breath. I don't know how long it went on, but it was the worst experience I went through. Suddenly, without any thought about it, I began wailing in strong tongues. Within ten seconds, I felt something break off me in the spirit realm, and I felt hungry. I had had no appetite for weeks. It steadied me. I did not eat much, but I ate something and felt stronger.

God spoke to me in His Word. I was supernaturally directed to the book of Hebrews. I opened right to the page, and I saw this in a caption above the scriptures there.

"Let God train you." Underneath it said,

> Therefore since we are surrounded by so great a cloud of witnesses, let us strip off and throw aside every encumbrance and that sin which so readily clings to and entangles us, and let us run with patient endurance the appointed course of the race that is set before us. Looking away to Jesus, Who is the Source of our faith and is also its Finisher. He, for the joy that was set before Him, endured the cross, despising and ignoring the shame, and is now seated at the right hand of the throne of God. (Hebrews 12:1–2 NLT)

I felt hope. First and most importantly, because it connected me to Kelsi. Second because it seemed God still had plans for my life, for His kingdom advancement. I did not see any plans ahead for me except to die in despair someday.

Soon after this, I woke one morning and became aware of a phrase repeating in my head.

"I bless you, Mom. I bless you, Mom. I bless you, Mom," I heard. I knew these were not my thoughts. The only person who ever called me Mom was Kelsi. I felt very comforted as God allowed another connection. This was not me seeking to "talk with the dead" as a medium does. I have no interest in such rebellious activities. It was another connection my very good Father allowed. I thanked Him with tears running down my face.

God reminded me of the day He pulled me up into His Presence a few years before. (This was referenced in my first memoir.) As I listened and recalled the experience, I felt some degree of the total blissful peace in the moment that I had felt back then. He said this was locked inside of me, like an imprint on my spirit, so that I could return to it anytime I chose to focus on that memory.

Nightmares became the norm. Horrible replays of our loss kept returning. I felt demonic assault on top of this, torment upon torment. Unresolved childhood trauma came out with a vengeance. God gave me two strategies. He told me to read Ephesians 6 and make sure to put on His armor every morning when I awoke and every night before I went to sleep. He also gave me a rhyme because I enjoy writing poetry. He said, "It isn't very hard to do before you go to sleep. Clean out your room with a very clean sweep." When I began using both of these strategies, things calmed down to a great extent. I simply told all evil to leave my house and to get off me, my husband, John, and our dog, Zoe.

Pastor Patricia Velotta, another friend and mentor, contacted me and offered to lead me through some Immanuel prayer sessions online. These encounters were extremely helpful. She encouraged me to abide with the Lord Jesus as much as possible.

Pastor Patti always encouraged me to focus on the Lord Jesus Christ while we prayed. He never leaves nor forsakes any of us. She has written a lot about using our godly imagination to become aware of and to see Him with us. "Find Him with you. Take a good look. He's right here. Take the extra step. 93 percent of communication is nonverbal. You receive much more information when you use your imagination to see Him. Imagination is the bridge between revelation and our thoughts. All our communication with Him comes through our imagination. The Greek word is *dianoia*. In the Bible, nine of the references to imagination are holy and four are evil. Imagination is like power, so allow Holy Spirit to bring the images to you. It comes into your thoughts. It will feel peaceful and biblical. Ask Him for help in this process. He wants us to hang out with Him, yet in our devotional times, we're often busy asking questions and looking at the scriptures and praying. He is here, and He wants us to abide with

Him. His name is Immanuel. This is His nature. He cannot change that. He is always with you," she reassured me.

I knew it was the only way I could move forward. It was a relief to focus on Jesus. It strengthened me. When I would receive a perspective change during the prayer time, I knew that was from God.

My other friend Denise walked through everything with me as faithfully as anyone could. When she heard from God that I was to take Kelsi's pictures down for a time, I obeyed. It gave me some respite from the pain to not constantly see her, though I continuously saw her in my mind's eye. Denise continued to pray with me every time I asked for help. I could not have endured Kelsi's funeral or the first several months without her constant guidance and support. She even prayed for a "quicker healing and better understanding and healing of all the trauma" than she had experienced when her son, Adam, moved to heaven. To pray for someone like that is to love them. Her prayers and loving support contributed greatly to my rapid healing.

Denise pointed me back to Jesus also. "Sometimes you will feel alone and want to die. Other times, you will feel the prayers of people and will feel grateful. You feel lonely, then you feel the love of Jesus and the protection of God. This is the deepest pain, to lose a child. It's like you are getting a PhD from Jesus. You will know Jesus will carry you through each moment where you don't want to survive. Just cry out, He is with you. I personally want to see something redemptive come out of losing Adam. I want to gain increased authority to help God's kingdom here on the earth. I want something in the end for God's glory. Not many people can do this. We paid the price, and will gain authority through this. The pain I went through over Adam was worth it. I did come to realize this was just what happened. We may never know why it did until the day we get to heaven. Then we won't care. The day will come that you will choose joy and life again."

When I said how much I missed Kelsi and her daily expressions of love toward me, Denise said it was just a part of my humanity. She redirected me to depend on the love of Jesus instead of a flesh love. When I described our daily hugs and loving relationship, she said we were both lucky mothers because not all moms had that with their children. I thanked God for the twenty-nine years I had with Kelsi. It was better to have learned to love deeply than never to have loved at all.

Denise reassured me that the deep pain would go away, and I would receive peace. "That hole never gets filled. It is not meant to be because it's who we are. Our children are a part of us. I don't want the joy of knowing Adam to go away. When I talk of him, I cry out of my love for him. It's not even the pain anymore. When you love deeply, the pain is also deep," she finished.

I also visited my older friend Joan who had lost her daughter and two grandchildren twenty-nine years earlier. Joan was a very loving encourager to me on this path. She agreed that "you continue to miss them, but you get better at managing the pain." Joan continued in active relationship with others into her nineties. She held Bible studies in her home and went on trips. She was another great role model. I am so grateful to God for positioning these wonderful women in my life.

One night, God said, "I'm in here to glue you to everything I am." The full understanding of this statement came a few months later.

We were attempting to get a video together for Kelsi's memorial service. As I looked at so many wonderful pictures, I kept breaking down. Though she still used the helmet, she managed to forget about OCD on our day trips. I have beautiful pictures of us parasailing together. She still smiles at me from a bench at Hershey Park Gardens, where we enjoyed the flowers after spending time in the Butterfly House. All those events were enjoyable. I loved spending time with her.

Then John asked if we really had to do the memorial service. He said, "Do I have to come?" I saw the pain in his eyes that mirrored mine. Suddenly, I thought, *Who am I doing this memorial service for?* It was not for us or for the rest of my family. I felt pressure to do it for others. A weight lifted off, and peace came. Kelsi didn't care if we did one or not. The people who truly loved her would remember her with fondness, and there was no need to push ourselves in our pain. We cancelled the service.

I had a very peaceful encounter in a dream. I had the understanding that somehow the grief process would be done "in half the time," and in fact, the healing was already happening.

As I heard God speak more frequently, I was able to *get away with* less. I was talking to one of my sisters about an older person who upset both of us. We were not seeing the person from heaven's perspective. God is a good Father and will discipline us in gentle but firm ways. I am very grateful for that. As I woke up the next morning, I heard a heavenly voice.

"Kelsi would like people of all ages to love each other," came through. I was not thinking about Kelsi in that moment, so I knew it was a message from God. I was convicted on a deeper level to honor God by loving others more. I believe the message came through that way because it got my attention very strongly. Kelsi loved people very much while she was here. She accepted them with ease. I would do well to emulate her character.

I read an excerpt from Latasha Morrison's book entitled *Be the Bridge*. She talked of the need to lament a loss, to express sorrow or regret. When we lament, we allow a deep connection to form between ourselves and the harm that was done to us. That first connection creates a pathway for healing and hope. She said, "We have to sit in the sorrow, avoid trying to fix it right away, avoid our attempts to make it all ok. Only then is the pain useful."[10] This confirmed my lament-laden worship and expression of all painful emotions. It brought peace to my soul.

It was only thirty days since Kelsi left. In two more days, I would be sixty-six years old. I sat quietly in my bedroom, practicing the Presence of Jesus. I kept my mind on Him with an attitude of gratitude and praise. Suddenly, I heard Him speak very loudly into my mind.

"You are MINE," He declared. I realized He delighted in me and rejoiced over me. I remained focused on Him. It is important to persevere in the act of abiding in His Presence. It takes practice at

---

[10] LaTasha Morrison, *Be the Bridge: Pursuing God's Heart for Racial Reconciliation* (Waterbrook, 2019).

first to slow your mind down. It becomes easier as you don't give up. Hearing Him this way enabled me to extend grace to others and even to myself. Jesus sees us in the middle of our messes, yet He also sees us perfected in heaven at the same time. He is with us in our pain but somehow greater than all of it. He knows who He created us to be and calls us forth to grow into that persona every day.

Now more strategies came forth. When a bad dream came, I was told to "meet that energy with Jesus Christ." I often heard to praise God when my thoughts went toward grief and darkness. This especially happened because of deep roots of self-blame for Kelsi's death.

Kelsi went through a stop sign on her bike and was hit by a car. I finally called the driver but could not get through to leave a message on her phone. I then called her husband's phone and explained I did not hold anything against her for the accident. I realized I blamed myself, which is why it took me a while to contact them. I was trying to avoid the excruciating self-guilt at the root. We had a brief but good conversation, and he appreciated my call.

I hung up and journaled for a while. God spoke.

"It's time for you to forgive yourself," He said.

Oh, it felt so wrong to do that. All the "what ifs" and "I should have knowns" rose up in a crescendo of self-rage as I sat there. But I knew that forgiveness was an act of my will in obedience to God. I did not have to feel like doing it. God engrained this into me years before. Perhaps a minute went by as heaven watched. As my emotions screamed inside, I knew I needed to move quickly in submission. I could not let my feelings rule me on this. I stood up.

"I now forgive myself, God," I said. At that very moment, I felt something like a shield clamp down strongly over my heart. I thought of the breastplate of righteousness in Ephesians 6, which is part of our daily armor, but this was something specific and additional, which God gave me because I obeyed Him so quickly. Stronger faith and love formed a protective covering over the pain, and it became very muted. It was a supernatural experience by the grace of God. It continues with me ever since and will be with me to my dying day. It was amazing.

Soon after that, God verified His power to heal me. "It is all a matter of My restoration," He said. I came to realize many more truths in the earliest part of the grief process. The things He spoke to me may offend people. If you have gone through deep grief, you may even think what He told me is wrong. In the earliest months, I did think He was wrong. But I came to be intrigued by what He said, and it brought me to deep and lasting healing. Remember, God's thoughts are not like ours. His ways and thoughts are higher. He is not encumbered by humanistic mindsets. He is the Only God, a Divine Being, and He thinks like One! When we struggle with some offense toward God, we do well to consider that He is the Creator.

> But who are you, O man, to answer back to God? Will what is molded say to its molder, "why have you made me like this?" Has the potter no right over the clay, to make out of the same lump one vessel for honorable use and another for dishonorable use? (Romans 9:20–21 ESV)

Deep in the recesses of our minds runs a self-negating commentary. This thread runs continuously and is not readily accessible to our conscious minds. By God's grace, He unveils these subterranean lies and then covers them with His mercy. He desires that we would see ourselves and others through His eyes of compassion and love. This is not to say He will not bring correction where we need it. He is too good of a Father to allow us to remain in sin. But He does this with exquisite care and tenderness. Only He knows the roots to our pain and sinful choices. He will bring the remedy to us as we listen, obey, and humble ourselves under His mighty hand. He will restore! Let hope and worship arise within you in a crescendo of awe and humility to Jesus, the King of kings and Lord of lords.

# CHAPTER 6

## The God of Surprises

It is important to know God loves you,
and to be anchored in His love.

—Beverly Blackwell

The last three months in 2019 were a blur. If I had not continued to journal with diligence, I would not have recalled any of it. Amidst all the excruciating pain of loss, God spoke to me about being His mouthpiece. He said wisdom would be released in the things I said and did. It was very hard for me to respond to most of what I heard. Only now can I appreciate how radically different His thoughts were from mine. Even during this earliest of time in the grief process, God urged me to come into alignment with Him. Honestly, I was put off by a move of His spirit inside of me within the first three months. Yet I knew my faith was developing in the midst of this extreme time.

My husband struggled with anger in his grief. I did also but received much healing when I just *let it all out* to God. I remember one time when I yelled and cried hysterically.

"How COULD You! How COULD You, God! You know what I was standing on! I believed she would be healed here!"

When my tirade ended, I felt incredible peace. I marveled at how good God is. He was not put off by my ranting. My husband suffered in silence. Then God reached out to him.

John came up to my work area and interrupted me, which was very unusual.

"Kathi, I have to tell you something. When I was in the shower, God told me that He could not heal Kelsi anymore here, so He took her home," he said. There were tears in his eyes. I was silent for a few minutes. I could see that the encounter had strongly affected and softened him. At first I thought, *But God can do anything!* Then I recalled these passages in the Bible where the people in Jesus's hometown took offense at Him because they "knew" Him.

> And coming to his own country (Nazareth), He taught in their synagogue so that they were amazed with bewildered wonder, and said, where did this Man get this wisdom and these miraculous powers? Is not this the carpenter's Son? Is not His mother called Mary? And are not His brothers James and Joseph and Simon and Judas? And do not all His sisters live here among us? Where then did this Man get all this? And they took offense at Him (that is, they were repelled and hindered from acknowledging His authority, and caused to stumble). But Jesus said to them, a prophet is not without honor except in his own country and in his own house. And He did not do many works of power there, because of their unbelief (their lack of faith in the divine mission of Jesus). (Matthew 13:54–58 AMP)

The last verse reads this way in a different translation,

> And He did not do many miracles there because of their lack of faith. (Matthew 13:58 NLT)

It is said a bit differently in the Gospel of Mark,

And He was not able to do even one work
of power there, except that He laid His hands
on a few sickly people and cured them. And He
marveled because of their unbelief (their lack of
faith in Him). (Mark 6:5, 6 AMP)

I remembered that even Jesus was hindered from moving mirac-
ulously here in the earth realm at times. In this case, their unbelief
prevented it. In other words, the spiritual atmosphere in Nazareth
was a deciding factor in preventing miracles. God is sovereign, yet
He puts Himself in a position where the behavior and beliefs of the
community may either bring life or death and stagnation. It was
not enough for me alone to have "enough faith" for Kelsi's healing.
Again, this is something I came to understand for our unique situation. There is another reference in the Bible where Jesus encouraged
a father to not fear when he heard his daughter had just died. He told
him to believe as He made his way to their house to raise her from
the dead. He removed people who were unbelieving from a room so
He could work a miracle.

And He allowed no one to follow him
except Peter and James and John the brother of
James. They came to the house of the ruler of the
synagogue, and Jesus saw a commotion, people
weeping and wailing loudly. And when He had
entered, He said to them, "why are you making a commotion and weeping? The child is not
dead but sleeping." And they laughed at Him.
But He put them all outside and took the child's
father and mother and those who were with Him
and went in where the child was. Taking her by
the hand He said to her, "Talitha cumi," which
means, "little girl, I say to you, arise." And immediately the girl got up and began walking (for she

was twelve years of age), and they were immediately overcome with amazement. (Mark 5:37–42 ESV)

Jesus removed unbelievers and scoffers from the room so He could work the miracle of resurrection.

I do not say this to condemn myself or my community. It is simply a sad connecting of the dots from the Word of God. Human beings are to respond to God's deep call within us to come to know Him and learn how to pray for those most sorely afflicted by evil, as Kelsi was. I imagine God saying this to us today.

"I desire to heal everyone. When My people are hard hearted, apathetic, or lukewarm, they prevent My miracles from coming forth. I need you to surrender to Me so that I may do mighty works of healing for the most severely tormented. I healed the Gadarene demoniac over two thousand years ago, and I am well able to pour through you to heal those with any mental illness. Repent of your doubt and self-sufficiency and come to Me and be healed. Together we will do the greater works that My Son Jesus spoke of."

We must become more humble, hungry, and teachable.

> Truly, truly, I say to you, whoever believes in Me will also do the works that I do; and greater works than these will he do, because I am going to the Father. (John 14:12 ESV)

This was a part of the puzzle of Kelsi's life. I believed I had faith for her healing, but many days, I was just worn down. I could barely look ahead to finishing out the day, let alone do intense spiritual warfare. God revealed more to me about His purpose for her life later on.

As I woke up one night, I had sad thoughts but began to praise and worship God. I was about to tell God how depressed and exhausted I felt. As I walked out of my bedroom, the Holy Spirit took control of my mouth. What came out of me were these words,

I surrender to Jesus Christ.

This was amazing because He actually moved my mouth with the words. He took charge of my lips. It was the oddest sensation. I then prayed a prayer of generational repentance for myself and all those in my ancestral line who never surrendered their lives to Him.

I had been telling God every night that I submitted to Him. I wondered why He used the word "surrender" in this case. God knows that I like to study the meanings of words, so He often uses intriguing phrases to draw me in.

The next day, I received His answer through a book by Brennan Manning called *The Importance of Being Foolish.*

> But there is an essential difference between submission and surrender. The former is the conscious acceptance of reality. There is a superficial yielding, but tension continues. It is halfhearted acceptance. It is described by words such as resignation, compliance, acknowledgement, concession. There remains a feeling of reservation, a tug in the direction of non-acceptance. Surrender, on the other hand, is the moment when my forces of resistance cease to function, when I cannot help but respond to the call of the Spirit. The ability to surrender is a gift of God. However eagerly we may desire it, however diligently we may strive to acquire it, surrender cannot be attained by personal endeavor.[11]

The worldly view of surrender is that it happens through personal striving and self-effort. It is always independence from the One true God that underpins all New Age beliefs. Various occult practices accompany the New Age followers. Here is a list of things to avoid. If you have practiced or even dabbled in them, admit it to God. Repent means to change your mind and turn back to Christ. If you need help to repent, find a follower of Jesus who will pray with you.

---

[11] Brennan Manning, *The Importance of Being Foolish.*

This list is not exhaustive but will start to set you free. Do not participate in fortune-telling, horoscopes, astrology, palm reading, tarot cards, pendulums, tea leaves, crystals, fetishes, charms, psychic readings, Ouija boards, table tipping, levitation, seances, clairvoyance, ESP, mental telepathy, channeling, the use of spirit guides, familiar spirits, communication with the dead, out of body experiences not sovereignly allowed by God, astral projection, reincarnation beliefs, psychic healing, powwow, magic, voodoo, sorcery, any type of Wicca or Satan worship, water witching, casting spells, incantations, divination, cursing, hexes, vexes, ungodly covenants, animal or human sacrifices. Repent and renounce for any known or unknown rebellion, deception, manipulation, intimidation, desire to control or desire to dominate others. Repent of any place you have used an evil spirit for any reason. Repent of witchcraft in all its forms.

New age beliefs originate in Gnosticism, which is a system of mystical religious and philosophical doctrines. Gnosis is knowledge of spiritual things that are known only to an elite few. Such knowledge touts itself as essential for salvation. Gnosticism says matter is evil and combines mythology, Greek philosophy, ancient religions, and eventually even Christian thought in an attempt to modify and alter truth. The Apostle Paul addressed the threat of this thinking in the book of Colossians because this doctrine had begun to infiltrate into the church there. Paul immediately corrected this and emphasized the preeminence of Christ. The death and ascension of the Lord Jesus was enough to save us. Everything that denies this is deception, evil, empty, and leads to futility.

In one New Age source, it is explained in this way,

> There are any number of ways to practice surrender—from softening your belly, to consciously opening yourself to grace, turning over a situation to the universe or to God, or deliberately letting go of your attachment to an outcome.[12]

---

[12] https://www.yogajournal.com/yoga-101/get-carried-away

This is simply another humanistic way of trying to explain and control something that only God can do. It strikes me as ludicrous that I could "soften my belly" and thereby accomplish surrender! We can't even "consciously open ourselves to grace," because grace is a gift from God too. He is the One Who opens us up to receive it! I find it ridiculous to turn my situations over to the universe because that is opening myself up to the evil realm. Those spirits will be happy to accommodate you and take you on the broad road to hell. Putting God in the mix here sees Him as another alternative to try instead of the only Way, Truth, and Life. Could someone practicing new age meditation feel they have "let go" of an attachment to an outcome? Yes, the spirits behind such practice are quite capable of lulling and deceiving people into a false peace. Jesus promises us something far superior.

> Peace I leave with you; My (own) peace I now give and bequeath to you. Not as the world gives do I give to you. Do not let your hearts be troubled, neither let them be afraid. (Stop allowing yourselves to be agitated and disturbed; and do not permit yourselves to be fearful and intimidated and cowardly and unsettled.) (John 14:27 AMP)

I want the peace of Jesus to pervade all my being. New Age practices put it back on humans to bring themselves into peace, bypassing the Creator! It's futile. We need to fall on Jesus as the cornerstone of God's salvation plan.

> Jesus said to them, 'Have you never read in the Scriptures: the stone that the builders rejected has become the cornerstone; this was the Lord's doing, and it is marvelous in our eyes? Therefore I tell you, the kingdom of God will be taken away from you and given to a people, producing its fruits. And the one who falls on this stone will

be broken to pieces; and when it falls on anyone, it will crush him. (Matthew 21:42–44 ESV)

Jesus spoke to the religious leaders of the day in these verses. The Pharisees had rejected Jesus as the Son of God. They rejected God's way of saving them. They relied on their knowledge of the Scriptures instead of recognizing the One Whom the Scriptures spoke of. When people believed in Jesus, they were convicted of their sins. They received Him as their personal Savior. In so doing, their old lives of self-reliance became broken, and they received the new, which was eternal life.

> You search the Scriptures because you think that in them you have eternal life; and it is they that bear witness about Me, yet you refuse to come to Me that you may have life. (John 5:39–40 ESV)

A Christian source was infiltrated with Gnosticism about what surrender means.

> A Christian does not need to "surrender daily" but to cooperate with what the Spirit of God communicates over the course of each day. Submission is a situational decision not a blanket declaration. You cannot submit your day to God. You can only submit as life rolls on throughout the day, anything else is pretending. Submission is relational cooperation done in the present tense. Submission is not tapping out because God twists your arm, it is tapping in, into the life, love, and relationship that God has given you with Himself. You cannot give your life to God. As a Christian God gave His life to you. He is your life (see Colossians 3:3–4). We are to simply walk with Jesus in newness of the new life

He has given us. There is no promise to make or achievement to grasp just trust God and His love for you as you live in Him and with Him.[13]

It is not that there is no truth to the writer's statements. I believe he is skirting a deeper issue here. If we do not need to surrender daily, then why did the Holy Spirit of God take charge of my lips to say it? Why did He lead me to focus on the need for it every day? I cannot get caught up in flowery words or philosophies any longer. I trust the raw intervention of the King. We need to surrender, and we cannot do it on our own. As we advance in relationship with the Lord through His great grace, He does it in us. We experience reality and weep with gratitude. Awe increases. Jesus is our Head. We come into deeper understanding of what this really means. We receive the insight that this isn't even our life to live on the earth. It is His life to live in and through us.

I repeat. Holy Spirit took control of my lips. I studied the difference between submission and surrender. I discovered it was a gift God gave to me. I could not surrender myself. He did it for me because He loves and owns me. Jesus is our best example of a surrendered life to the Father.

So Jesus said to them, "Truly, truly, I say to you, the Son can do nothing of his own accord, but only what he sees the Father doing. For whatever the Father does, that the Son does likewise." (John 5:19 ESV)

Then God told me, "It starts with passion, that's what you want to pray for." My online *Merriam-Webster Dictionary* defines *passion* as "the sufferings of Christ." It also calls it "the state or capacity of being acted on by external agents or forces." It can refer to emotions that may mean intense, driving, or overmastering conviction about

---

[13] love-god-love-others.blogspot.com/2011/11/surrender-or-submission-defeat-or.html

something. Ardent affection as in love and an object of desire or deep interest are the remaining applicable designations for this word.

In my concordance, this word covers a broader swath. The Greek word used in the New Testament means to experience a sensation or impression, which is usually painful. It means to suffer, to feel things deeply. Jesus suffered as He laid down His life at the hands of evil men who were also antagonized by the evil one. He is our role model of how to handle this.

> When He was reviled, He did not revile in return. When he suffered He did not threaten, but continued entrusting Himself to Him Who judges justly. (1 Peter 2:23 ESV)

> For because He Himself has suffered when tempted, He is able to help those who are being tempted. (Hebrews 2:18 ESV)

As followers of Christ, we must expect to experience human suffering. Jesus told Ananias to heal Saul, who became the Apostle Paul after He was blinded by a dramatic encounter with Jesus on the road to Damascus.

> For I will show him (Saul) how much he must suffer for the sake of My name. (Acts 9:16 ESV)

The spiritual ideal we are to realize is found in identifying with Christ in the passion of His crucifixion.

> Since therefore Christ suffered in the flesh, arm yourselves with the same way of thinking, for whoever has suffered in the flesh has ceased from sin so as to live for the rest of the time in the flesh no longer for human passions but for the will of God. (1 Peter 4:1–2 ESV)

The Word also tells us the whole Body of Christ suffers when one member suffers.

> If one member suffers, all suffer together; if one member is honored, all rejoice together. (1 Corinthians 12:26 ESV)

Passion includes feeling vexed by demon powers. One reason God could want us to experience this would be to overcome and destroy them in our lives or the lives of others. That is love, to suffer the effects of an evil external power for the sake of setting someone else free.

In obedience, I asked Him to kindle His passion in me in the middle of the horrendous pain.

The holidays were very hard. Early in the month of December, God did something so unexpected I could not digest it. In the early hours of the morning, this is what happened.

The Holy Spirit suddenly engaged with my spirit and rose up on the inside of me. "It's a joy to serve Jesus! I can't thank Him enough," were the words I heard. I felt an intense thrill as His great joy leapt up inside. It was another very surreal experience. My soul, which is my mind, will, and emotions, was flat and dead in the water. My spirit felt Him, but my soul could not respond. It made no sense to my mind, coming this soon. To be totally honest, I felt repulsed. I journaled the experience but actually ignored it until God addressed it.

I was trying to watch a football game with John a few weeks later. I have never had any interest in the sport but wanted to sit with him, and he wanted to watch it on TV. As I listlessly tried to get the rules straight in my head, God spoke.

"You think it's disloyal to feel My joy this soon after Kelsi came home," He said. What a great kindness in that He did not refer to the feeling of repulsion. He linked that emotion to my underlying belief about myself. I felt I would be a bad person, even a traitor to Kelsi by accepting His joy within three months of her passing. I did not say anything out loud. I remember nodding in agreement and respect. God always nailed it.

It took another few months until I recognized that God didn't think it was disloyal or too soon to have me experience His joy. What was I to do with that? Any human being would believe it wasn't right to feel that way at that time. Yet that's when God moved with joy. I decided I needed to align with Him.

I practiced God's presence through meditation on Him and His word. I always asked Him to guide every thought, memory, image, emotion, and physical sensation coming into my awareness in leading my imagination when I sat quietly before Him. He is worth waiting for!

Suddenly, the Holy Spirit showed me Jesus standing next to my bed in a very vibrant way. He was much bigger than what I had seen in my imagination previously. He had on a white robe and He was smiling. He held my hand and said, "Beloved, I will never leave you. Maintain obedience."

Then God encouraged me even more.

"Look at Me on the inside of you," He said. I began to practice this form of contemplative prayer. Saint Theresa of Avila was a fifteenth-century Carmelite nun who practiced and taught this simple process. It involves focusing on the Godhead inside of one's being, perhaps slowly saying the Lord's Prayer or any other pertinent scripture that keeps one's mind on God. I said, "God I want to see You inside of me." He answered quickly.

"Come! Rejoice!" He exclaimed.

It was Christmas Eve. I got ready to go to my sister's house where all the family would gather. I felt dread to go through this holiday because it had always been Kelsi's favorite one. The thought came to me to ask God for a special present.

"God, this is so heartbreaking for me. Kelsi is with you, and I am doing my best to rejoice because You told me to, but it still hurts so much. Would you please give me a gift before I go over tonight?"

God answered within an hour. His voice was very gentle.

"I am delighted to have her here with me," He said. It went through me like warm honey.

"Thank You so much, God. Now I can participate with the family," I said.

God loves to communicate with us in different ways. In the New Year, He sang into my spirit, which is attached to His, "Every day, every day, the future gets brighter every day," in a bright little tune. I kept receiving everything in faith and felt stronger with each connection. I brought my will into alignment with His and persisted in praising Him.

There were still very hard days. Kelsi was ever-present with us for twenty-nine years. She did not get the chance to leave the home due to the oppression she experienced. Though I heard from God frequently I could not open her bedroom door for seven months. I usually avoided even looking at it.

Beverly, my friend from Arizona who heard from God about Kelsi, texted me great encouragement, "Don't be so hard on yourself. It's a healing journey. Some days you feel you have accepted that Kelsi is in a better place, that she is really happy and singing with the angels and dancing with Jesus. Other days you can't understand why this happened, or why you weren't warned. You think you didn't pray enough or maybe something was wrong with your walk with God. In all the questions you are trying to make sense out of it. You probably will not get answers to most of them. It is important to know God loves you and to be anchored in His love. You need to know His character and rest in His love. He works all things together for our good. He knows everything at all times, from the beginning to the end of all things. Rest in His arms, if you can. He really loves you!"

I heard a preacher say that the power to create is to frame your world with the words that we speak. I did my best to say God's Word over my life on a daily basis.

I received comfort from Marty Cassidy, a leader with Chuck Pierce at Glory of Zion church in Corinth, Texas. I had worshipped online with this community for several years. Marty said that she lost her only child twenty-five years ago. When she asked Holy Spirit how to bear it, His Presence came vibrantly next to her in the bed and said He would be her holy best friend. She also said a turning point was here and that what the enemy did for our harm God intended to turn it for good. She said God was dealing with the backlash of the enemy through His angelic forces. These prophetic messages gave me hope.

God cautioned me to dwell in faith when things got rocky. He took me to His Word.

> So that Christ may dwell in your heart through faith. And I pray that you, being rooted and established in love, may have power, together with all the saints, to grasp how wide and long and high and deep is the love of Christ, and to know this love that surpasses knowledge—that you may be filled to the measure of all the fullness of God. (Ephesians 3:17–19 NIV)

I truly believe that the Word of God washes us and creates new neurological pathways in the brain. It is not just words on a page. When we read the Word of God, we are interacting with Jesus. His light gets inside, and physical change occurs.

My friend Denise encouraged me to start working again in January 2020. I moved forward in faith. God held me and those I counseled in His very capable hands.

Dr. Jim Denison writes *The Daily Article*, which is a Christian online email addressing tough cultural questions of our day. In one of his emails, he wrote,

> God gives us strength, spirit and courage to bear up under life's sufferings. Sometimes He removes the pain, sometimes He does an even greater work of giving us strength to endure it. Either way it is a miracle.[14]

God knew when my thoughts would start to wander down grief's pathway again. I felt my strength waning one day as the same old thoughts began to trickle into my mind.

---

[14] Jim Denison, "The Daily Article," Denison Forum, www.denisonforum.org.

"Grief consumes. Keep your eyes on Me," the Lord said. Then He sang another tune, "Oh so marvelous, Oh so clear! Jesus is wonderful, Jesus is here!"

This interaction supercharged me to a new level of worship.

I read about something called "toxic positivity." The author cautioned against forcing oneself to be happy when one was not. I considered this in the midst of all my God moments. I knew I had been in the pits of hell with grief. I had not avoided it. I was not in denial. But I knew the Word of God and that it is infallible. I believed Kelsi had moved to heaven, so I did not grieve as a nonbeliever would. For this, I am eternally grateful and hope my book will bring others to the saving knowledge of Jesus.

> But we do not want you to be uninformed, brothers, about those who are asleep, that you may not grieve as others do who have no hope. For since we believe that Jesus died and rose again, even so, through Jesus, God will bring with Him those who have fallen asleep. For the Lord Himself will descend from heaven with a cry of command, with the voice of an archangel, and with the sound of the trumpet of God. And the dead in Christ will rise first. Then we who are alive, who are left, will be caught up together with them in the clouds to meet the Lord in the air, and so we will always be with the Lord. Therefore encourage one another with these words. (1 Thessalonians 4:13–17 ESV)

One morning, the Holy Spirit intensified my focus on God to the point that I felt exceedingly glad and on a spiritual "high." Some charismatics refer to this as being drunk in the Holy Spirit. The glory of Jesus inside of me lasted through most of the morning. This greatly increased my motivation to focus on Him. Maybe God preempted another grief wave that morning so that it could not consume me.

My sister Jan had a beautiful encounter in a dream. I recorded her encounter and share it now just as she emailed me.

> I hope it's okay that I let you know about this dream. I had a very real encounter, dream, whatever you want to say, last night. In my dream Kelsi was there with all smiles on her face, and she so happily and proudly said to me, "Look at me now!" It was quite a joy filled moment and I was all smiles and sort of woke up and had a great smile on my face and felt great peace.

I had been crying because I just separated out some of Kelsi's clothes from mine. I knew Jan had a God encounter. I wondered if perhaps God healed her of the trauma of having to tell me by phone about the accident. I wondered, with awe, what Kelsi looked like healed! Her face would have been in total peace. My brain went tilt, again. It was hard to imagine her with the mind of Christ. After twenty-four years, she now lived fully restored, without torment!

> For now we are looking in a mirror that gives only a dim (blurred) reflection (of reality as in a riddle or enigma), but then (when perfection comes) we shall see in reality and face to face! Now I know in part (imperfectly) but then I shall know and understand fully and clearly, even in the same manner as I have been fully and clearly known and understood (by God). (1 Cor 13:12 AMP)

Another person saw Kelsi standing outside near our driveway with her arms to the sky. Light was shining on her face, and the person was overcome with peace. I was very glad to hear of these connections allowed by God.

Many writers encouraged me. Gregory Dickow is a pastor who wrote this in an email,

> There are over 1000 predictions or prophecies in the Bible, promises God made before they happened. The chances of only 17 coming to pass are 1 out of 450 billion x 1 billion x 1 trillion! Yet all the promises came to pass! God's Word is true whether you feel it or not. He has kept all His promises and has never failed. I am in God's presence by the blood of Jesus, so because He is with me I fear no evil. God loves me perfectly which casts out all my fear. I have power, love and a sound mind in Jesus's Name![15]

I was filled with awe pondering this message. Yes, Kelsi now has a sound mind. I determined to continue to meditate on God's Word and flood my mind with His love thoughts. I would dwell on the reality of God living within me.

One day, I asked John a question.

"John, why do you think Kelsi's words were 'I'll see you soon, Mom' instead of goodbye?"

John said, "To give you comfort. If they have no time in heaven, maybe it will be like a blink of an eye for her when you get there." His words assuaged my soul.

Kelsi and her best friend Patrick texted each other on every holiday. He missed her very much, as did her other friend, Kayla. I kind of became a substitute for her. I loved communicating with them, and sometimes it also hurt. Yet I so appreciated when people remembered her. On Christmas Eve, I told my niece Ellie how pretty she looked. Ellie brought Kelsi right into the moment.

"You know, Kelsi always said, if it's a holiday, you better be dressed up for it. It's not worth having the holiday if you don't," she said. It made me laugh. I felt sad yet warm at the same time.

---

[15] Gregory Dickow, pastordickow@changinglives.org.

Brutal insomnia and nightmares dogged me for months. God cautioned me to "be careful going up on pills" when I was tempted to increase the over-the-counter herbs. When I would focus on Him again, it often got me back to sleep.

I chose joy again. One night in February, in a time of silent worship, I had this thought, *Jesus, I am in You. You are in me. I am redeemed, and I am Yours.* I got a very fast response from heaven.

"Say it!" God said. I knew He meant He wanted me to say it out loud, so I did. Right after that, I was thinking about writing this book but could not come up with a title. I went through several possibilities in my head over an hour or so and fell back asleep. As I woke up, I heard God speak in the deepest, most gentle voice I had heard to date.

"Choose joy, beloved," He breathed into me. I was ecstatic!

"Wow, God, that is a GREAT book title! Thank you," I blurted. Then I realized something.

"Oh, You're actually saying that to ME. You want ME to choose joy and keep doing it. It's still a great title though," I said. It made me laugh again. Yes, it became the title of this book, and it was God's passionate love drawing me ever closer to Himself.

It is also God's message to all of you reading this book. Choose joy, beloved. Choose Jesus inside of you and grow into a passionate, on-fire relationship with Him. It's why you are here.

# CHAPTER 7

# The Teacher and Comforter

God uses broken things. It takes broken soil to produce a crop, broken clouds to give rain, broken bread to give strength. It is the broken alabaster box that gives forth perfume. It is Peter, weeping bitterly, who returns to greater power than ever.

—Vance Havner

I turned my attention increasingly toward God. The Holy Spirit became my lifeline.

In the Gospel of John, chapter 14, Jesus introduced His disciples to this amazing third Person of the Trinity. He said the Father would send another Comforter after Jesus went back to heaven. He was preparing them for what was to come.

Jesus said this Comforter was the Spirit of Truth Who would live with them constantly and would also be in them. The Greek word for *Holy Spirit* is "parakletos," which means an intercessor, consoler, advocate, or comforter. According to the *Strong's Concordance*, it means,

The one summoned, called to one's side, especially called to one's aid and is used of the Holy Spirit destined to take the place of Christ with the apostles after Christ's ascension to the

Father, to lead them to a deeper knowledge of the gospel truth, and give them divine strength needed to enable them to undergo trials and persecutions on behalf of the divine kingdom.[16]

Jesus said this,

But the Comforter, (Counselor, Helper, Intercessor, Advocate, Strengthener, Standby), the Holy Spirit, Whom the Father will send in My name (in My place, to represent Me and act on My behalf), He will teach you all things. And He will cause you to recall, (will remind you of, bring to your remembrance) everything I have told you. (John 14:26 AMP)

The Holy Spirit represents Jesus and teaches us all things. He even causes us to remember things Jesus said. As I typed this book, scriptures came to me as Holy Spirit encouraged me to include them. As a believer, you have the best teacher in the world inside of you.

But when the Comforter (Counselor, Helper, Advocate, Intercessor, Strengthener, Standby) comes, Whom I will send to you from the Father, the spirit of Truth Who comes (proceeds) from the Father, He (Himself) will testify regarding Me. But you also will testify and be My witnesses, because you have been with Me from the beginning. (John 15:26–27 AMP)

---

[16] James Strong, "Greek Dictionary of the New Testament," *The New Strong's Expanded Exhaustive Concordance of the Bible: Red-Letter Edition* (Thomas Nelson, 2001), 190–190.

The Holy Spirit cannot lie. He only tells the truth and testifies about Jesus. We are to partner with Him because we also know the Lord and can exhort others as we speak of His workings in our lives.

> However, I am telling you nothing but the truth when I say it is profitable (good, expedient, advantageous) for you that I go away. Because if I do not go away, the Comforter (Counselor, Helper, Advocate, Intercessor, Strengthener, Standby) will not come to you (into close fellowship with you); but if I go away, I will send Him to you (to be in close fellowship with you). (John 16:7 AMP)

Jesus said it is to our advantage that He left because that was the only way the Holy Spirit would come to all who believe. We have access to Him at all times. He leads us in the way we should go.

> And when He comes, He will convict and convince the world and bring demonstration to it about sin and about righteousness (uprightness of heart and right standing with God) and about judgment. (John 16:8)

It is the job of the Holy Spirit to convict people of the sin of unbelief. He convinces and shows, by demonstration, how to live right because Jesus was no longer here in the flesh to do so.

> But when He, the Spirit of Truth (the Truth-giving Spirit) comes, He will guide you into all the Truth (the whole, full Truth). For He will not speak His own message (on His own authority); but He will tell whatever He hears (from the Father; He will give the message that has been given to Him), and He will announce and declare

to you the things that are to come (that will happen in the future). (John 16:13, AMP)

We see that the Holy Spirit only says what He hears from the Father. He does the same things Jesus did. He is Jehovah-Nigad, the Lord Who predicts the future. He always gets it right.

The Holy Spirit has a tremendous job to do here on the earth. When we believe in Jesus and receive Him into our hearts, the Holy Spirit is ignited and comes to live inside us. We have the best Counselor available to us, free of charge, at any time of the day or night, for any problem! He is on continual standby! He prays when we do not know what to pray. He stands up for us as our strongest Advocate. We realize we cannot do life in our own strength any longer.

Every time I open the Bible, I ask Him, the glorious Spirit of Truth, to speak reality into my life. He opens my eyes afresh and anew to passages of Scripture that I have read many times. He is Light within us. Truth is illuminated as we study with Him. The Bible is not like other books, which are words printed on pages. His Word ignites fire within our being. They supernaturally reach into our hearts, and we change. As a child of God, you have constant access to the best Teacher there is.

If you want to receive Jesus as your Lord and Savior, tell Him exactly that today. You may pray to receive Him through a pastor or any believer, or you may even pray alone. Here is an example,

> Lord Jesus, I believe that You came in the flesh through the virgin birth to destroy the works of the evil one. I believe You are fully God and fully Man. I believe that You died for my sins and were resurrected to eternal life on the third day. I thank You for saving me from death, and I receive You today as My Lord and Savior. Thank You for reconciling me back to Father God so that I now have access to Him in unbroken relationship. I ask You to fill me with Your Holy Spirit.

*Lord, as they pray this prayer, I know You will meet them and bring them into Your kingdom!*

God kept speaking and I kept listening. One night, He said, "Some do the works of Christianity, and some long for the Son and freedom." I knew He wanted us to desire Jesus and come out of the bondage of ungodly religious works into deep relational liberty and truth. I had done those works, striving to be good enough for Him, for many years. Now I simply yearn deeply for more of Him. Out of this place of intimacy will flow the works He has designed for all of us to do from before the foundation of the world.

"Eventually your heartbreak ends. I need you to walk in love," God said. I had a hard time believing my broken heart would heal, but I set my faith in that direction. I knew He meant I was to continue to grow in love toward others until it was my time to go home to heaven.

When I saw Kelsi in dreams, it was beyond painful. In one dream, Kelsi came walking toward me in my mother's kitchen. I was overwhelmed with joy.

"Kelsi, Kelsi!" I cried out with delight. Immediately, the Holy Spirit surrounded me. I felt his peace.

"No, she's not here," He said with deep compassion. I kissed her cheek.

"Kelsi, do you know how much I love you?" I asked. I woke in tears.

I wanted to ask God about her but could not even frame a complete question in my despair.

"God, does Kelsi know?" I stopped.

"Everything," He said. Oh, His voice was so gentle. Because I connected with Him, I felt sad but not passively suicidal as before. His presence always saved me.

I had to watch my words so grief would not overtake me. As I talked with Denise, I began a sentence with the words "when Kelsi died." She immediately corrected me with the words "moved to heaven." I used that phrase from then on. I continued to make the conscious choice, moment by moment, to think God's thoughts of joy. I still ask for God's grace to thrive every morning before my feet hit the floor.

I have had many sessions of generational deliverance and inner healing over the years. I could not lead others in this process if I were not willing to endure it myself. In March of 2020 during a session, I felt I was sitting on top of a furnace as God did some interior cleanup. I felt stronger but still overwhelmed when I focused on not seeing Kelsi here any longer. At times, that pain went so deep I could not talk. That's often when I heard God come in the closest.

"I love you," He whispered. "I am your future and hope, Kathi. Come to Me and rest."

I studied and took notes on what God's rest was. In Hebrews 4:9, the Greek word for "rest" refers to a perpetual sabbath rest which meant uninterrupted fellowship with God. It was not necessarily referring to a weekly day like Saturday or Sunday, although it is holy and wise to rest one day per week. The rest of God Himself is where we may enjoy an indissoluble relationship with Him. In Hebrews 4:10, the word "rest" means we stop believing in our own works. It does not mean we don't work. It means we are peaceably assured within and in our outward lives about God's daily provision as we do His works.

The Pharisees were enraged because Jesus healed people on Saturday, their Sabbath. Jesus did this deliberately. He wanted them to engage with a higher principle. Although it is good to have a day of rest, the idea was not to just refrain from activity, but to do good, even heal, on any day, including the Sabbath. The actual intent of a Sabbath day was to bring rest and well-being to humanity. If that included helping another human being, which created activity of some kind, God was okay with that. God even made allowances within the law in the Old Testament because priests still performed their duties on the Sabbath.

There is a "here now and not yet" consummation of rest, but we strive to enter it now. We need faith in Jesus, and we are to enjoy being established in God's presence. As we worship, we may partially enter into the end-time rest by recognizing Christ's finished work of redemption.

In Hebrews 4:11, it tells us to strive to enter God's rest, which means we are to persevere in believing in the good news of what Jesus accomplished for us by His death and resurrection. If we refuse to persevere in this, we disobey.

Hebrews 4:12 tells us God is the Word and the Word is God. It is His personal utterance to us and is living and active. It exposes our thoughts and intentions constantly. This is a very good thing because we then recognize when we need to repent. This brings us back into the rest of God.

God had told me to teach about joy before Kelsi's accident. I taught two lessons in 2019 before it happened. He asked me to finish the study in 2020. This was a daunting task to undertake but only if I looked at myself. If I kept my eyes on Jesus, I was fine. I came to understand why after I watched an internet conference from Life Model Works called "Thinking with God: Weaving God's Thoughts into Human Identities and Relationships," hosted by author and teacher Jim Wilder. He studied the implications of attachment love for spiritual formation. He talked of the central importance of our need for healthy, loving attachment to parents. In a download, Mr. Wilder explained as follows,

Attachment love forms a kind of permanent "glue" uniting two people. The human brain is pre-wired to glue/attach itself to the source of its life. Thus, the one who feeds us, gives us our drink, or gives us shelter will become the center of our attachment love. In Hebrew the word dabeq (to glue) is used which commands us to attach permanently to God (i.e., Deuteronomy 11:22). Letting the serpent feed us was an attachment mistake. Asking the Baals to feed us or provide fertility creates attachments to them. Those who feed on words of life, eat the Bread of Heaven, drink Living Water and dwell in the shelter of the Most High also build attachment love. The love that attaches us to the source of life is attachment love.[17]

He had me at the word "glue."

I suddenly understood what Holy Spirit said to me several months before. "I am in here to glue you to all that I am." God desires to bond us to Himself. He needs to be our principal attachment figure. This is good news for people who did not have healthy connections with parents. It brings such hope. Many times we form healthy attachments with surrogate parent figures, and that is fine. When we turn more to God and see Him as our ultimate perfectly good Papa, everything changes. This takes time, especially if there are many wounds from childhood. But it works.

Most deep understandings of reality come to us through suffering. I became desirous to share God's heart and pray for His desires to develop in others. This brings joy to Him. He told me He couldn't wait until I could see more clearly what was in His heart for His children.

I began to have an increased number of eye flashers and floaters. Denise had a word from God and helped me to pray for healing, and they stopped. As I entered into worship, I heard God say, "Pen," so I picked it up and wrote what I heard.

"I am coming to deliver, heal, defend, restore, recompense, reinvigorate, repair, rebuild, revitalize, and remake this nation. I am your Mighty One and you are My beloved. Turn and return to Me with all your hearts. Let Me do a deep work in you. I will sovereignly bring Mine to Myself, count on it! Passion for Me is what you want. Ask Me for this, and you shall have it. Believe and hold onto Me."

I asked God how to pray.

"Together," He said. This may start from a prayer list and move into joining in His flow. I found that more thoughts and situations, even nations, came to me in prayer as I gave Him more of my time and attention.

---

[17] James Wilder (director), "Thinking With God: Enhancing Our Immanuel Lifestyle," lifemodelworks.org/thinking-with-god/.

Diane Nutt is a pastor of a nondenominational church in Rockwall, Texas. She has a very deep relationship with God. I listened to her three-CD set entitled *Keys to Your Glory Encounters* many times for a few months. She said this about the "secret place" referred to in Psalm 91,

> It's a haven. You cultivate a heart for His presence and create a place where He comes down and rests. His love fills your home. You set your heart apart for Him through obedience. Don't shrink back because no one else paid the price for you! God causes us to triumph and overcome so we master sin through Christ. When we overcome sin a specific fragrance of Christ is manifested and comes through us. Thank God because He will cause you to triumph through Christ, through the anointing inside of you. Abide in His word daily. His Truth makes you free. Present your body as a living sacrifice to Him whether you feel like it or not. The more you do, the more God loads you with benefits.[18]

Michael Koulianos is a spirit-filled pastor who wrote a book entitled *Jesus*. He was also one of the speakers at the Arizona conference I had attended in August of 2019. He happens to be Benny Hinn's son-in-law, and I was deeply impacted by his passion for the Lord. Michael exalts Jesus over and over and is deeply in love with Him. I highly recommend his book.

The Word came alive to me. Meditating on it increased my awe for God. It saved me one night from a very difficult supernatural encounter. After I went to bed, I began having severe stomach pain and pressure. After fifteen minutes, I began to get out of bed to awaken my husband. Then God spoke.

---

[18]  Diane Nutt, *Keys to Your Glory Encounters* (CD set).

"Awareness of these powers now subsides," He said. All the pressure stopped immediately. I was learning how to sense the unseen realm around me. Powers in high places were exerting pressure on me. Suddenly, I recalled the Word of God. Remember, it is alive and full of power!

> (Jesus) has now entered into heaven and is at the right hand of God, with (all) angels and authorities and powers made subservient to Him. (1 Peter 3:22 AMP)

I knew that everything was subservient to Jesus. I was under His authority. By extension, powers or other things in the unseen realm could not hurt me either. I was so filled with faith about this that I knew such an experience would not be repeated. I also knew that if I came out from under Jesus's authority, they could hurt me. We need revelation and understanding from God in order to navigate in that realm.

God told me joy was returning even after a bad dream, which usually included a self-blame loop. Denise said this cycle was a derivative of the masonic in my bloodline. Old mindsets and blind spots take time to change. I felt a strong internal shaking on this one evening. God counseled me to "remain still." I trusted Him to do whatever was necessary on the inside.

The thought came to me to begin to memorize more scripture. I began to study the book of Ephesians. As I read verse 11 in chapter 4, God interrupted my study.

"It was He who gave some to be apostles, some to be prophets," I began. Before I could finish the verse, the Holy Spirit interjected a word that startled me.

"Martyrs," He added. I stopped.

"What? Why did You just say that?" I asked Him. I knew apostles, prophets, evangelists, pastors, and teachers were part of God's fivefold ministry team, which is supposed to build up the Body of Christ in order that believers may do the works of God. I was mystified. I marked the word in my Bible and did a study on this.

One of the definitions of the word *martyr* is "victim—especially a great or constant sufferer." As a verb, it refers to "torture." It comes from the Greek *martyr* which means "witness." The word became associated with dying for religious beliefs because so many early Christian witnesses were persecuted or killed.

I found that the Apostle Paul made reference to martyrdom in a discussion of the spiritual gifts in 1 Corinthians 13:3. He said we may give all we possess to the poor and surrender our bodies to the flames in an act of martyrdom. If we do this without love, we gain nothing by it.

Many prophets in the Old Testament were killed for speaking the words of God to the Jewish community. After Jesus's death and resurrection, the apostle Stephen was the first martyr mentioned. He was stoned to death for his belief in Jesus. All of Jesus's disciples except John were martyred through beheading, crucifixion, beatings, killed with axes, or torn in pieces by animals. All these men loved the Lord God and died for Him. This was precious in God's eyes.

In my studies, I understood that martyrdom was indeed a specific spiritual gift. I did not connect the dots about why He said it to me in Ephesians 4:11 that day. Sometimes things have to percolate while you continue to ask, seek, knock, and grow more in love with Jesus.

A few months later, it hit me. I believe God meant that Kelsi was a martyr, and it was somehow for the sake of His kingdom. She fit the definition. She suffered constantly and greatly for most of her life. That torture was especially heinous during her last two years here. During her whole life, no matter how much she suffered, she never turned her back on Jesus. She was a living witness for Him. She was not physically beheaded, but her mind was taken from her through vicious assault on a daily basis. If what I came to understand was true, then she fulfilled her purpose on the earth. It still hurt to lose her, but I began to see that God's plan was so much larger than anyone could see. Unless He chooses to divulge truth, we will not know it. I never would have come to such a conclusion had He not interjected His word at that moment I was memorizing the scriptures. The Holy Spirit is our best Teacher.

Then I encountered Father God in a dream. A nice man whom I thought was a pastor sat with me in my childhood bedroom. He asked why I take so many notes when I study. I explained when something is important to me, I really go after it and want to establish it in my mind. He gazed at me and said He appreciated that about me. I smiled and thanked Him so much for all His teaching. He became tearful, and I woke up. Because the dream setting was in my childhood home, I knew God was showing me that He was always with me. A God encounter will leave you refreshed and full of wonder. I felt how soft God's heart is toward us. Later He told me I could enjoy His heart as I studied His Word.

God shares in our pain. He came so close to me in my darkest moments that He saved my life. I could feel His compassion and comfort for me. Since going through such great loss, I am able to extend His love to others as they go through the valley of the shadow of death.

"My Body is hurting," He said one day. In obedience, I finished teaching the Joy Bible Study. I then began to send out emails to the group who had attended. God exhorted me to continue doing this. I became aware of how much others needed to know that He wanted an intimate relationship with them. I wrote about intimacy out of my daily life with Him.

I became aware that the increase of God's word in me was causing me to grow in holiness.

"You will give and give and give and receive My greater and greater glory," God said. I came to see that giving comes out of our covenant relationship and is linked to our worship. We don't just give money, tithes, and offerings. When we give worship to Jesus as King, He takes His stand on our behalf. When we serve and bless others, we give to Him. Do not hold back from giving out of what God has entrusted to you. We need to receive from Father and give to others from that place. We manifest His presence as we do so.

The Holy Spirit is the Spirit of glory, and there are three levels to experience. The first is called the doxa glory, referenced in Matthew 25:31 and in 2 Corinthians 3:18. In the latter, it says we move from one degree of glory to another. You become very sharply aware of

Jesus's presence as King in your atmosphere. The second level is called the Shekinah glory, and this is a visible glory. An example of this is seen by the cloud by day and fire by night in Exodus chapter 40. I saw this on the face of Mr. Hunter, the elderly man with the healing ministry in Texas. His face actually shone with God's glory. The final type is called the Kabod glory, where you can feel the weightiness of God. I describe experiencing this last type of glory in my first book for about one hour in my home. At that time, I knew God was there but didn't know what it meant. In my home church, nobody had such experiences that I knew of, so I had to seek information from other sources. We should want to see and move in God's glory, as Moses desired. Miracles happen in God's glory.

One simple way God's glory comes through us is by being friendly to others. Kelsi had that down pat. She would talk to people all the time, complimenting them on their clothing or their children.

I was still plagued by memories of seeing Kelsi in the ER at the hospital. Denise explained how God showed her to rejoice that Adam, her son, was now with Him in heaven. I then saw myself back in the room at the hospital. I looked up and smiled that Kelsi was no longer in torment. She was in absolute bliss with Jesus. Denise said the enemy would want to continue to torture me with memories. God showed her a remote control device. He told her to "turn it off" when the enemy did that. I learned to say, "Jesus, I want to use my imagination now to turn that memory off." I didn't need to keep doing that due to the level of healing I kept receiving from God. It was truly amazing.

"Deactivate all demonic channels and activate the heavenly frequency," God said. I did this in faith. I wanted to receive from Him. God told me His heart was very tender and He yearned for His people. This changed my prayer life.

We were coming up on two anniversary dates I was dreading—Mother's Day and Kelsi's birthday. Some years, they were on the same day. This year, her birthday fell on the day after Mother's Day. I prayed and asked God for protection.

CHAPTER 8

# Holidays, Memorial Stones, and God's Loving-Kindness

*God's faithfulness is the one constant in the
equation. He is the Rock on which we stand.*
—Paul Silway

The day before Thanksgiving 2020, I sat down to rewrite this chapter to get it ready for publishing. The phone rang. It was Missy, the salesperson from Weaver's Memorials.

"Mrs. Basehore, Kelsi's tombstone was finished and was set at her grave site today," she informed me.

I was not surprised. She had told me it would probably be completed in November of this year, but I did not expect to receive the news on the eve of the Thanksgiving holiday. God's timing is always perfect. Would I continue to give thanks to Him? As I looked at this chapter heading, I just shook my head in wonder. Yes, God, I will praise You in the storm. I know it is the only way to ride it.

> I will offer to You the sacrifice of thanksgiv-
> ing and will call on the name of the Lord. (Psalm
> 116:17 AMP)

"Yes, thank you so much, Missy," I said. It was dark outside, so I knew I had to wait until the morning to see it.

Six months earlier, I remember asking God for special protection for Mother's Day and Kelsi's birthday, which were one day apart in May. God outdid Himself. He wrapped His arms around me so close that both days were calm and peaceful. My niece Ellie gave me a funny Mother's Day card, and it warmed my heart. On Kelsi's birthday, I bought some new plants and birdseed at a nursery. We had friends for dinner, and it was fine. I was shocked at how easy both dates came and went.

It had been nine months since Kelsi's funeral. I finally felt strong enough to order her memorial stone in June. John, ever supportive, was ready to do it when I was.

"John, what shall we put on her stone besides her name and dates of birth and exit?" I asked, feeling overwhelmed again.

John looked down as he often does when he is listening for God. Then he tentatively smiled at me. "See you soon?" he asked. I was overjoyed!

"That's perfect! I would not have thought of that!" I said through my tears.

"Well, that's all I heard you saying for months. You walked around the house, crying, repeating, 'See you soon, see you soon, Kelsi,'" he reminded me. It was true. God allowed me to see her words, and they provided a rock-solid foundation of trust. Ahead, in our future, we will be with Jesus and Kelsi forever!

Denise agreed and added this idea. "Can you imagine how it will raise the faith of people walking through the cemetery when they read those words?" she said.

John and I prayed together before we went to the cemetery. This was the first time either of us had returned since her burial. Power is released in us when we stop avoiding things. It also helped to bring about more closure and acceptance. We needed to do this before we went to choose her tombstone.

"Are you ready?" John asked as we looked at the burial plot. I saw the family names already lying in rest there. My father, his mother and her second husband, and my paternal great aunt's names rose before us. They had all lived far beyond the age of twenty-nine.

"Yes, let's go. I'm ready," was all I said. We drove to the display room and began the process.

I felt the Lord protect us as we looked at all the drawings and designs. Scroll or open book? Which flowers should we use? My brain started to crumble.

"What would she have liked?" John asked.

Immediately we both said, "Roses." I was so grateful for his guidance. It brought me back to the present task and steadied me. In the end, we agreed it went much better than we anticipated. We still quickly moved to the door upon completion. It was enough for one day.

Then Memorial Day rolled around. To my surprise, I experienced much more heaviness and grief than the double anniversary dates two weeks before. This particular holiday had never affected me to this extent. I realized that having been so sensitized to the loss of our daughter, I was now also extremely aware of others who were grieving losses of their loved ones on this day. I began to pray for these hurting people. The Bible tells us we are to bear each other's burdens. Burden bearing is a special gift from God, which allows us to feel the pain of others. We then lift that pain up to God as we intercede until God releases the burden.

> Bear (endure, carry) one another's burdens and troublesome moral faults, and in this way fulfill and observe perfectly the law of Christ (the Messiah) and complete what is lacking (in your obedience to it). (Galatians 6:2 AMP)

We need to have courage to live this life. We need mental and moral strength to persevere. Courage means guts and fortitude. The origin comes from a French word for "heart" and refers to the emotional and moral nature, our innermost character. It means we will venture out especially in the face of danger. A synonym for *courage* is "adventure," which involves unknown risks. I recalled God's words spoken through Kelsi one day as we were halted at a stop light.

"Mom, the idea of an adventure, whatever kind it is, even on a vacation, is to experience the good and the bad. It's how you get to know things. Some parts of a vacation can be unpleasant, but what do you expect? It's supposed to be a safe haven? The idea is to live a real-life adventure. You learn from the good and the bad," she said.

As she spoke, the weight of her words hung heavily in the atmosphere. There was a holy hush following this simple but profound truth. God wanted me to get this.

"Kelsi, that is awesome! I never thought of it that way. You're right, an adventure must include elements of danger or pain. It's not all fun and games," I said. The light finally turned to green, as though moving forward had been contingent upon my reception of that truth.

As I thought of writing this book, I realized that to share all the things God told me took courage. I had to decide to be vulnerable and risk people disapproving of and judging me or my spiritual experiences. If anyone judges me for what God has told me to write, I forgive them. He told me not to fear people's faces, attitudes, or judgments. I must only fear and obey Him. No matter the turmoil we go through, He was and is present with us. He never abandons us. I will show two translations of the latter portion of Hebrews 13:5 and also verse 6 to illustrate how emphatically God promises this.

> For He has said, "I will never leave you nor forsake you." So we can confidently say, "The Lord is my helper; I will not fear; what can man do to me?" (ESV)

> For He (God) Himself has said, I will not in any way fail you nor give you up nor leave you without support. (I will) not, (I will) not, (I will) not in any degree leave you helpless nor forsake nor let (you) down (relax My hold on you)! (Assuredly not!) So we take comfort and are encouraged and confidently and boldly say, "The Lord is my Helper; I will not be seized with alarm

(I will not fear or dread or be terrified). What can man do to me?" (AMP)

Many times, the Amplified translation has branded my heart. When something is amplified, it is expanded through use of additional details. God's promise comes through with much greater intensity and strength as we read the second translation. It increases our sense of safety in Him.

God is ALWAYS present. We cannot escape Him even if we want to. I am so grateful for that.

> Where shall I go from Your Spirit? Or where shall I flee from Your presence? If I ascend to heaven, You are there! If I make my bed in Sheol, You are there! If I take the wings of the morning and dwell in the uttermost parts of the sea, even there Your hand shall lead me, and Your right hand shall hold me. If I say, "Surely the darkness shall cover me and the light about me be night," even the darkness is not dark to You; the night is bright as the day, for darkness is as light with You. (ESV)

Thank You, Father God, for Your Word. Thank You for sending Your beloved Son, Jesus Christ, to die for our sins, resurrect the third day, and reconcile us back to You! Thank You that as we believe in Jesus, we are sealed as Yours and will be in eternity with You! Please let this truth burn into the souls of anyone who does not yet know You. Save them, Father. You are not willing that any should be lost and go to hell.

> The Lord is not slow to fulfill His promise as some count slowness, but is patient toward you, not wishing that any should perish, but that all should reach repentance. (2 Peter 3:9 ESV)

Repentance means changing one's mind. It means to turn away from evil and turn back to Jesus.

God asked if I was "urgently expecting" Him. He said I needed to be dependent upon and committed to Him. In other words, even if He does not return in my lifetime, I am to live each day as though He may return at any moment. The Bible talks about the virgins who had sufficient oil in their lamps so when the Bridegroom came, they were able to go into the feast with Him. Oil is a metaphor for Holy Spirit. Jesus meant we must keep a vibrant lovesick-dependent relationship upon the Father, burning with Holy Spirit's passion every day. We must keep our minds tuned in to hear the voice of Jesus. In this way, we will enter into the kingdom of God.

> But at midnight there was a shout. Behold, the bridegroom! Go out to meet him! Then all those virgins got up and put their own lamps in order. And the foolish said to the wise, Give us some of your oil, for our lamps are going out. But the wise replied, There will not be enough for us and for you; go instead to the dealers and buy for yourselves. But while they were going away to buy, the bridegroom came, and those who were prepared went in with him to the marriage feast; and the door was shut. (Matthew 25:6–10 AMP)

Live each day as though it will be the one the Father chooses to have Jesus return.

God is the same yesterday, today, and forever. He is still the burning bush, aflame with love for us. I promise, You want His love. You want to be lovesick. It is the best thing in the world. You want to pant for Him like a deer pants for water in a desert. Lukewarm, "correct" joyless behavior in church is not God. We should be on fire for Him. He is worthy! We are only here because He created us! Glory to His Name, the matchless Name of Jesus!

We were made to worship Him. If we do not worship Him, we will form false idols. We will bow down to them and ourselves.

Make no mistake, you will worship something. It feels wonderful to worship God. The hardest thing for me personally is when I keep my eyes on myself. I will either fall prey to the gutter balls of pride or false humility. False humility means to focus on and denigrate self. It's a form of pernicious idolatry. True humility is knowing that everything is about Jesus. It's a relief to stop focusing on self. When I put my eyes on Jesus and adore Him, I feel the awe of God. You want that too.

The study of awe is on the rise in the literature. It is defined as

> An overwhelming feeling of reverence, admiration, fear, etc., produced by that which is grand, sublime, extremely powerful, or the like: in awe of God; in awe of great political figures. Archaic: power to inspire fear or reverence. Obsolete: fear or dread.[19]

Research suggests that awe can make you happier, healthier, more humble, and more connected to the people around you. It may sharpen our brains, reduce materialism, and make us less impatient. It may increase generosity and make us more cooperative with each other. [20]

I found three Hebrew words in the *Strong's Concordance* that refer to the word "awe." I will refer to two of them here.

> Let all the earth fear the Lord (revere and worship Him); let all the inhabitants of the world stand in awe of Him. (Psalm 33:8 AMP)

This word means to dwell or sojourn in a land. It can mean to turn aside from the road to lodge somewhere as a guest. It also can

---

[19]  https://www.dictionary.com/browse/awe

[20]  About the Author Summer Allen, "Eight Reasons Why Awe Makes Your Life Better," Greater Good, greatergood.berkeley.edu/article/item/eight_reasons_why_awe_makes_your_life_better.

mean to shrink, to fear, to dwell, abide, stand in awe, or remain. As we worship the Lord, we continue in our focus upon Him. We abide or remain in this place. The longer we abide, the more we are transformed into the image of Jesus.

> Princes pursue and persecute me without cause, but my heart stands in awe of Your words (dreading violation of them far more than the force of prince or potentate). (Psalm 119:161 AMP)

This second word means to be startled due to a sudden alarm, to fear in general, to feel awe, or to shake.

I had a few experiences of awe connected to God's presence. It went far beyond what I felt while gazing over the Grand Canyon in Arizona. These moments with God only lasted a few seconds. I was in a time of worship with eyes open in total darkness. Suddenly, a tiny light opened up and enlarged to perhaps a circumference of ten inches. Just as quickly, it shrank and disappeared. In the split second of enlargement, I knew I glimpsed Jesus in His glorified state, and I gasped, shaking. He was breathtaking!

With those experiences in mind, I concur with the definitions from dictionary.com and with the two Hebrew words noted in the Psalms. I love to see the beauty of nature, but give me awe for the Person of God Himself any day!

In the Bible, *heart* and *mind* are synonymous. Whomever or whatever you focus upon will enlarge in your life. If you focus on the news, your heart will become full of despair. If you focus on God, you will be filled with peace and hope despite events highlighted by the media. God may then bring His news to your brain. He may desire for you to pray for another country, for example. There may be dire things going on there, and your prayers are effective fuel to change events. You will feel energized after these prayer times because they connected you to God.

> Therefore, confess your sins to one another and pray for one another, that you may be healed.

The prayer of a righteous person has great power
as it is working. (James 6:16 ESV)

This verse not only teaches that righteous people have powerful prayers. We also see the connection of confession of sins to healing. When we confess our sins to a trusted person, they are to pray for us so our minds become clear, and positive changes will occur. Sometimes there are curses that come against us, which have to do with unconfessed sins in our generational lines. If we step forward to repent for recurring evil behaviors, thoughts, and attitudes, the operation of curses coming against us will be stopped.

I previously referred to Derek Prince, now deceased, an excellent preacher and teacher. In his book entitled *Blessing or Curse: You Can Choose*, he outlines seven indications that a curse is operating in your life. These include the following areas:

1. Mental and/or emotional breakdown
2. Repeated or chronic sicknesses (especially if hereditary)
3. Barrenness, a tendency to miscarry or related female problems
4. Breakdown of marriage and family alienation
5. Continuing financial insufficiency
6. Being accident-prone
7. A history of suicides and unnatural or untimely deaths

This is a great resource to learn how to take action against curses in the unseen realm.[21]

Pastor taught on the necessity and value of repentance. I have heard some current teachers say it is not necessary. I don't see how our minds will change if we don't participate with God in this. I discovered that I needed to comprehend and feel the effect of my sin on God's heart. This is what brought me to true repentance and lasting

---

[21] Derek Prince, "Seven Indications of a Curse," *Blessing or Curse: You Can Choose* (Chosen Books, 2006), 53–53.

change. God's kindness leads us to repent. How can others teach we do not need to do this?

> Or do you presume on the riches of His kindness and forbearance and patience, not knowing that God's kindness is meant to lead you to repentance. But because of your hard and impenitent heart you are storing up wrath for yourself on the day of wrath when God's righteous judgment will be revealed. (Romans 2:4–5 ESV)

In fact, if we do not lead a life of ongoing repentance as we seek God and He reveals truth to us, we have impenitent hearts. We are not contrite. It would be like a murderer saying he would do it all over again, given the chance. This leaves us on the awful receiving end of God's wrath, which is reserved for the unbeliever.

> The Lord is close to those who are of a broken heart and saves such as are crushed with sorrow for sin and are humbly and thoroughly penitent. (Psalm 34:18 AMP)

I read a book by Dr. Kevin Zadai called *It's Rigged in Your Favor.* In his book, Dr. Zadai said God told him to ask a group of pastors what they would do in life if they knew they couldn't fail?[22] I was pondering this question myself, and I heard God say, "You're not going to, in your heart." I felt great relief. He did not say I would never do anything wrong again. He said no matter what happened, He had my heart, and I would prove faithful to Him.

Our carnal minds fight against our spirits. I found myself starting to think of nostalgic memories about Kelsi, and God intercepted them.

---

[22] Kevin L. Zadai, *It's Rigged in Your Favor: How Would You Live If You Knew You Wouldn't Fail?* (Destiny Image Publishers, Inc., 2020).

"Wisdom," He said. I knew He meant I should just keep my thoughts on Him. I obeyed.

I heard a Scottish prophet in Emma Stark's leadership group testify this during an online class, "I pray you will have the courage to go on an adventure with God, to the deep places of revelation; that you will have courage to pursue God and to pursue His Word. You will come out of your current realm of comfort. You will become all God intends for you to be." That tied in God's courage word with Kelsi's "adventure" word. God will confirm what He is saying to you. As you read this prophecy, you may agree and claim it for yourself.

"How do I yield to You, God? By faith?" I asked.

"And through My loving-kindness," God answered. There it was again, the sovereignty and greatness of God. Everything begins and ends in His grace.

You may ask God about anything. For example, I thought of all the worldly beauty seen in Broadway shows. I wondered how a production would look if spirit-filled Christians would write, produce, and act in them.

"There would be sound, vibration, and healing that would occur," (to people in the audience) He said. That is so much greater than simply being entertained by talented actors.

A few months before Kelsi left the earth, God multiplied money in our safe. I put several hundred dollars in there, mostly $50 and $20 bills to save for vacation. Right before Kelsi and I went to the shore, I went down to retrieve some. I opened the safe and pulled out the envelope. As I retrieved the cash, I was amazed. There were fifteen $100 bills in there!

"John, John, come here! Did you put this cash in the safe? What's going on?" I yelled as I ran upstairs waving the bills.

"No, you know I can't open that thing," he said. He looked closer. "Those are freshly minted bills. See the blue stripe on them?" I compared it to an older bill. He was right, no blue stripe. It took a while for it to sink in. God multiplied the cash. No one else had access to the safe. I was the only one who ever opened and closed it.

We received it as a miracle and thanked Him. After Kelsi was gone, I decided to sow it into whatever God told me to. I knew He would multiply it in some way for His kingdom purposes again. The number 1500 means light, power, and authority in biblical understanding. I wanted His light, power, and authority to come through me as He saw fit.

As I continued to listen, God said I needed to train my brain to think differently in order to align with His thoughts. He spoke to me in terms of being a watchman for Him. I was not very familiar with this term but soon received fuller understanding. A watchman is a type of prophet who sees ahead, things both good and bad, and warns or exhorts the specific community about them. Watchmen intercede, receive revelation, prophesy, and make decrees, watching after God's Word so they will see it manifest. The power of Holy Spirit inside activates the revelation. He uncovers what is not yet seen. I believe there are many watchmen on the walls who don't know it yet.

God was accelerating my training in the supernatural realm. I tell you these things to encourage you. He will do this for anyone who shows interest in Him.

I still missed Kelsi so much. Even knowing she was no longer in torment was not enough some days. One day I walked through the grocery store. Suddenly, I heard a young man talk to his mother.

"I love you, Mom," he said. I gasped as I felt a dagger cut into my heart and tears came to my eyes. Kelsi had said that to me all the time! I was not expecting this. I quickly made my way to the cash register. The clerk cheerily said she enjoyed seeing my mask that was decorated like a dog's face. I rallied to talk with her. On my way out of the store, a beautiful little girl waved and smiled at me. I winked at her through the pain.

Once home, I longed again to go home to heaven just to see her. Through my tears, I yelled, "I just miss her, God!" Soon afterward I opened an email from the Scotland prophets. I include parts of it here,

> Stop weeping, oh chosen one! Don't you know the authority that is already within you? Don't you know the roar of the Lion of Judah that brings victory over your situations and cir-

cumstances? The Lord is raising in you a roar—the roar of the Lion of Judah. The roar of God from within you will bring breakthrough and will bring healing of anxiety and depression to your whole family. He will clothe you in His oil of gladness and joy and worship will spring up from you like never before!

I was freshly astounded how quickly God answered me through His Beloved. Again, the prophetic word brought me strength and comfort.

The pull to remember Kelsi was not as strong, but my mind wanted to turn to thoughts of her. One day as I thought of writing this book, I knew it would cover the time of the latter part of 2017 through the year 2020. I found myself repeating the words, "Her last two years, her last two years," and the sadness began to overshadow me. Suddenly, God interrupted me.

"ON THE EARTH," He stated. It hit me like a lightning bolt of relief and joy.

"Oh, that's right, God! Thank you so much for reminding me of truth and helping me again! You save my life every day," and I cried, but these were tears of joy.

The truth is this. I was in the wailing pits of grief-hell about Kelsi, but God interrupted and showed me His truth. God came right into the worst trauma I ever experienced and taught me about grief, joy, and trusting in Him. He told me the future gets brighter every day. He opened my eyes to the unseen realm and allowed me to see Kelsi's words the day after the accident. He allowed me to feel Kelsi rubbing cheeks with me. He opened my ears to hear Kelsi blessing me. I did not ask for nor believe I could have such experiences, but they saved me. God is sovereign. He extends mercy to whom He will. It brought me back from wanting to die to choosing life.

I would not necessarily say to another grieving parent the things God said to me, but I would pray this, "Lord, let them know You, turn to You, and hear Your gentle voice. Let them receive Your comfort and truth about their child. Enable them to survive what feels unsurvivable. Teach them to thrive in spite of it. Amen."

Thanksgiving morning 2020, I woke up. I was both eager to see Kelsi's tombstone and avoid it. Tears began, and I let them flow as I prayed. God's steady presence filled my heart. Remember, my heart whispered, "She is not there." She is joyous in heaven in her spirit body. Kelsi is actually doing great! Because Jesus is alive, and she is His, she is alive right now! John and I drove up very early to beat the rain. It was cloudy and damp outside.

"There it is," I said softly. I got out of the car and carefully looked at it.

"It looks very pretty," John said. I was glad we had chosen the roses on top and the open-book style instead of the scroll for the words.

It's perfect, I thought. The rose-colored stone stood out brightly against the other black and gray ones surrounding it. Kelsi always loved color.

Beloved Daughter
KELSI ALLEGRA BASEHORE
May 11, 1990–Sept 27, 2019
SEE YOU SOON

# CHAPTER 9

―― ✺ ――

# Joy, Endurance, and Extravagance

So comes snow after fire, and even
dragons have their endings.

—J. R. R. Tolkien,
*The Hobbit or There and Back Again*

There is no escaping it if you are going to grow in joy. You are also going to suffer, one way or another. These two things are inseparable. This morning, the day I sat down to rewrite this chapter, worship rose up in me to such an extent I could only exalt Jesus. I called Him my Savior and my King, and suddenly, the Holy Spirit spoke through my spirit.

"He is My Joy," I heard. God has been the Hound of Heaven with me about joy. From a few months before Kelsi moved home to be with Him and until the present, I have heard His voice and experienced surges of ecstasy. Joy is a person. It is Jesus manifesting His Presence and power through our spirit. During the fill-up phase, it feels tremendous. I am strengthened and empowered for the day.

And Do not be grieved, for the joy of the
Lord is your strength. (Nehemiah 8:10 ESV)

As God calls on us more and more to bear the burdens of others with Him, sadness comes. There is no avoiding this because God feels sad for His beloved people who suffer. We will feel His heart for them as we partner in love. It is part of our calling to do this, to share in their good times and bad.

> Rejoice with those who rejoice, weep with those who weep. (Romans 12:15 ESV)

> Bear one another's burdens, and so fulfill the law of Christ. (Galatians 6:2 ESV)

In the morning, I felt the joy surge as Jesus refilled me. In the afternoon, I spoke to a man whose wife had just died. He had autism and lived in a boarding home. I felt God's love for him as we spoke. After we hung up, I asked people to give him a Christmas card shower. Then I cried. I thought of all the lonely people who had lost loved ones in 2020 and must get through "the firsts" of each holiday without them. God wants to use all of us to love on others. We are to provide for each other's needs, whether physical, emotional, or spiritual.

"Look at Me on the inside of you," God encouraged. I focused on Him in prayer, in His Word, and in others. When He began to draw me in closer in worship, everything changed. Now I look for Him to manifest Himself in me everywhere I go.

> You are the light of the world. A city set on a hill cannot be hidden. Nor do people light a lamp and put it under a basket, but on a stand, and it gives light to all in the house. In the same way, let your light shine before others, so that they may see your good works and give glory to your Father who is in heaven. (Matthew 5:14–16 ESV)

God told me I could choose joy very early on in the grief process. Because I obeyed, that journey was supernaturally shortened to an amazing degree. There was still deep pain during the first seven months, but God intervened, and things shifted rapidly. I have no other explanation. There is no human rationale to decipher the extraordinary healing and stability I received.

God linked three words together for me in this chapter. They are joy, endurance, and extravagance. We will begin with definitions of joy.

The Hebrew language is much more expressive and meaningful than other languages. When we think of joy in English, we do not have the expansivity we find in Hebrew. To further enlighten our understanding, I have included Hebrew meanings for *joy* from the Old Testament. I have also shown Greek words for *joy* from the New Testament. These are all taken from the *New Strong's Expanded Exhaustive Concordance of the Bible.*

In Nehemiah 8:10, the word for *joy* is "chedvah." It refers to rejoicing and gladness.

There are four OT verses that use the same Hebrew word for *joy*. These are found in 1 Samuel 18:6, 1 Kings 1:40, 1 Chronicles 12:40, and Ezra 3:12. It is the word "simchah." It has many meanings including "blithesomness," which means to be gay, merry, upbeat, buoyant, and chipper. It also means glee, which is to be strongly happy and feel great pleasure or satisfaction. This is exultant high-spirited joy and comes from an old English root "gleo," which refers to entertainment and music. Mirth is the next meaning, which gives us the idea of gaiety with laughter. The old English root is from "merry" and synonyms are festivity, hilarity, merriment, and joviality. This word also means to rejoice, which is to feel joy and delight or give joy to, or to gladden exceedingly, to an extreme degree. Synonyms would be fierce, great, immense, incredible, mighty, and intense. This particular word takes rejoicing "over the top."

In Esther, we have the word "sawsone." It is cheerfulness, showing special welcome, gladness, and mirth.

Ironically, the book of Job has three different words for joy. First is "mawsoce." One takes delight very concretely in the cause or object or it can mean abstractly feeling the emotion of joy. The second is "rawnan" where one may shout for joy, sing aloud, sing for joy, and cry out. The idea here is exaltation that demands loud singing in praise to God. The last one is "terooaw" referring to clamor, an acclamation of joy or a battle cry, clangor of trumpets as an alarm, shouting, an alarm sound, loud noise blowing, and jubilee. One of Job's friends, Elihu, says if one sees God's face when he prays to Him, He will have this type of "alarming" reaction. In Job, we especially link up the idea of joy with suffering.

In Psalms 21:2, the word "sawmakh" means to brighten up, cheer up, and usually refers to spontaneous emotion or extreme happiness expressed in some visible or external manner. This emotion arose at festivals, circumcisions, weddings, or harvest feasts or when Israel overthrew its enemies. There is a visible expression with this word. (In Jeremiah 50:11, the Babylonians are denounced as being jubilant over the pillage of Israel, and their emotion was expressed externally by skipping about like heifers and neighing like stallions.) Emotions may be accompanied by dance, singing, or musical instruments. This is a spontaneous unsustained feeling of jubilance, a feeling so strong it must be expressed externally and is prompted by an external stimulus. The action is focused on the subject. God is sometimes the subject, the One Who rejoices and is jubilant as in Psalms 104:31.

"May the glory of the Lord endure forever; may the Lord rejoice in his works." Does that modify or intensify your idea of what God is like?

From Psalms 30:5, we know "joy comes in the morning" and means a shout of joy (or grief), a proclamation, a triumph.

"Gheel" means to exceedingly rejoice "unto God my exceeding joy" in Psalms 43:4

Joy in Isaiah 65:14 is "toob" and means good in the widest sense, goodness, the best, beauty, gladness, and welfare.

In Habakkuk 3:18, joy means to spin around under the influence of any violent emotion, whether rejoicing, delight, or cringing in fear.

We may summarize what *joy* means in the Old Testament. It can mean rejoicing, gladness, gaiety, using music, hilarity, being fierce, feeling delight, shouting, clamor, or trumpets sounded as alarms when God's face is seen. There are spontaneous expressions of emotion with dance or singing in reference to external situations like feasts. It also includes proclamations of triumph, the best in goodness, gladness, welfare, and even spinning around under violent joy.

Here are a few of the Greek words in the New Testament for joy.

In Matthew 2:10, the word is "kharah." It means calm delight even when one falls into trials (as seen in James 1:2) because one is cooperating in the authority of the Lord. This is the reference most used in the new covenant.

When the babe leaped for joy in Elizabeth's womb in Luke 1:44, the word is "agalleeasis." It means he welcomed Jesus and felt exultation and exuberant joy. We also see this in Jude 24, Amplified Bible, where it says, "Now to Him Who is able to keep you without stumbling or slipping or falling, and to present you unblemished before the presence of His glory in triumphant joy and exultation (with unspeakable, ecstatic delight)."

I love that verse. Jesus keeps us from falling. He will present us, spotless in His glory. As He does this, His triumph and joy will be almost unspeakable. He will feel ecstatic delight. I believe this because I feel ecstasy when He fills me up.

"Yoofrosoonay" is found in Acts 2:28 and means to be of good cheer and have gladness of heart.

Romans 5:11 uses the word "kowkhahomahee," which means to boast or glory as Paul said, "We joy in God."

Philemon 7 uses "charis," which means gratitude, grace, favor, or thanks. Paul expressed much gratitude toward Philemon because he was such an effective witness for the Lord Jesus. When we see how great God's grace is toward us at all times, our gratitude should overflow to Him. God is extremely friendly toward us.

The word "oninemi" in Philemon 20 means to benefit or profit. In this verse, Paul is confident Philemon will show brotherly love and forgiveness toward Onesiumus who had run away from him. This brought Paul joy.

My favorite word is "agalliao" found in 1 Peter 4:13. Here *joy* means to jump for joy, and it is also found in Matthew 5:12 where

Jesus spoke of how great would be their reward for suffering, because the prophets before them were also persecuted. It is also found in Luke 1:14 in Mary's song about God's great favor to her and also in John 8:56 when Jesus spoke of Abraham's joy in seeing His day.

We will be rewarded for our suffering that we endure for God. The Apostle Paul suffered tremendously, yet he called his beatings, stonings, and shipwrecks "light afflictions."

> For this light momentary affliction is preparing for us an eternal weight of glory beyond all comparison, as we look not to the things that are seen but to the things that are unseen. For the things that are seen are transient, but the things that are unseen are eternal. (2 Corinthians 4:17, 18 ESV)

In the New Testament, joy is more frequently connected with suffering and persecution as more mature believers faced greater challenges in the early church. Joy became a character trait refined by the opposition. In other words, their joy grew despite their circumstances. Definitions include calm delight even in the face of trials. We are to cooperate in His authority. Joy is exulting in Him, having glad hearts, boasting in Him, feeling gratitude, receiving His grace and friendship, benefitting and profiting as we see His brotherly love expressed toward others even when betrayed and jumping for joy.

When I felt Holy Spirit rise up in me exclaiming "it's a joy to serve Jesus," it felt most like the word "simchah" to me. He was extremely upbeat and high-spirited compared to my deep emotion of grief at that time. As I progress in choosing joy every day, I connect mostly with the word "kharah," calm delight, or "charis," feeling gratitude and thanks toward God. This morning before the rewrite, I felt agalleeasis, an exuberant joy I could barely contain.

Our next concept is endurance, which is tied to joy. In our first reference, Nehemiah 8:10, the word "strength" means that we can endure and resist being moved or broken by the enemy. When we endure, we take a stand, like a soldier on watch. We arise or engage in battle. We bear up courageously with patience, to the end. It may mean to forebear or hold up against a thing and so bear with it. We endure afflictions and are born along by the Spirit's power. God's presence inside, His joy, is the fuel for endurance.

We don't lose heart. We persevere bravely in misfortunes, and we are longsuffering. We are slow to anger. There is a level of patience that only grows through trials. Should we suffer undeserved trouble, it brings glory to God. As we continue to bear fruit for His Kingdom, we run our race effectively.

If we are to endure, we must withstand any hardship without yielding. Sometimes this is necessary to sustain a prolonged stressful effort or activity. Synonyms include ceaselessness, continuation, persistence, and abidance. John and I have been called to endure our lives here without Kelsi's presence. The deep unspeakable heartbreak has subsided, but we must still endure. We watch others enjoy the presence of their children. This continually abides and will not change. The key to thriving in our lives is that we have adopted God's perspective. She has indeed simply gone ahead of us. We will be with her forever in heaven. God's daily presence comforts and sustains us.

Jesus is our role model of how to endure the worst of circumstances. He focused on the "joy set before Him," as He saw all of us who would believe on His name, forward into eternity. As we emulate Him, we encourage others to endure. One older saint, Joan, who had lost her daughter and two grandsons assured me, "People are watching how you handle your loss of Kelsi." I was able to receive this from her because she had to endure great grief. She was a wonderful example to me. In the same way, I need to be this for others.

We must decide to set our faces resolutely toward God's eternal purposes for others on the earth. We are to love to the end of our time here. Set your heart toward Father God's plans and purposes for your life and for theirs.

How and why does God Himself endure?

> I know that whatever God does, it endures
> forever; nothing can be added to it nor anything
> taken from it. And God does it so that men will

(reverently) fear Him (revere and worship Him,
knowing that He is). (Ecclesiastes 3:14, AMP)

Whatever God does, He puts His whole heart into. His staying power is ceaseless, is continual, and endures any adversity without yielding. It lasts eternally. God endures for humanity's sake. As He endures with us, His hope is that we will come to believe He is, and that we will learn to worship Him.

The Lord is not slow to fulfill his promise as
some count slowness, but is patient toward you,
not wishing that any should perish, but that all
should reach repentance. (2 Peter 3:9 ESV)

Jesus endured scoffing, spitting, and His beard was pulled out. He was scourged to the point that He looked unrecognizable. He was separated from the Father and betrayed by those closest to Him. He held on "for the joy set before Him," which was to see us come into His kingdom as explained in Hebrews 12:2. We are His joy. He lights up when He sees us.

"Dogs teach people unconditional love," God said. If you have a dog or cat, you know how they jump for joy after you have been gone for two minutes. God's joy is so full when we finally decide to spend some time with Him. Yet He gave us pets because they give us a human experience of His love. He is so good! I love my dogs, and I appreciate their loyalty to me, but their joy does not compare to experiencing His when I worship Him.

God put action on my heart to sustain joy in the face of grief. As I obey Him even in writing this book, I know it bears everlasting fruit for His kingdom. I will endure because my God endures, and I worship Him. Like everything else about Him, God's endurance is extravagant.

It is the best thing for us to worship God. When we revere Him, it means we show devoted deferential honor and know God is worthy of it. Synonyms include adore, deify, glorify, and worship. To worship means to honor and show reverence for God as the Divine Being He is. It is to both highly regard and express an action toward

Him that shows great respect, esteem, and devotion. We are to show extravagant admiration to God. When we worship, we idolize, adulate, or dote on Him. To dote means we show God excessive attention, fondness, or affection. Worship is an extravagant response to an amazing God.

*Extravagant* means exceeding the limits of reason, lacking moderation, balance, restraint, or extreme elaboration. The idea of profuse and lavish apply here. It could seem exorbitant, even insane to show such worship. Jesus's death on the cross was the ultimate extravagant act of love where He totally poured Himself out for us.

God is the most extravagant Giver of all. He gave us Jesus! Would any of us give one of our children to die for anyone else? No, we would not. Yet God did this! Nonbelievers see Jesus's execution on the cross as beyond the limits of reason. They disdain it as excessive and intolerable. Without any understanding of God or His Word, they decry the need for the ultimate blood sacrifice of Jesus because they do not see the depravity of their sin. Hanging onto that mindset will take them to hell. The world is a war zone, and God has redeemed all of us who come to Him through His Son. *The Power of the Blood* by H. A. Maxwell Whyte is well worth a purchase to open the eyes of our hearts. The reason we have access to God the Father is because of the sacrifice Jesus made on our behalf. To drive home this point, the Holy Spirit made a comment one day.

"He was murdered," He said, as I was thinking about Jesus in prayer. It made me gasp. I knew He was killed for our sakes, but when God applied the correct term, it became the horror that it was for me. Jesus was unlawfully killed, with malice aforethought. It was an outrageous and blameworthy action. He had not done anything to deserve it. We did. As a noun, a synonym for *murder* is "hell" and an antonym is "heaven."

Extravagant love expressions on our part toward God will enable, strengthen, and change us. God is looking for this from us.

Jesus loved how Mary broke her alabaster box and poured her precious ointment over His body. The event is recorded in all four gospels. In Matthew 26 and Mark 14, Jesus said she did a noble, beautiful thing to Him and prepared Him for His burial. He promised that wherever the gospel is preached, that event would be told in her memory. In John 12, it is recorded she also wiped Jesus's feet with her hair. In those days, people anointed and used perfumes frequently, but this particular action of using her hair is the reckless exceptional gesture here. In Luke 7, there is more emotion recorded as she also wept and kissed His feet.

How would we react if we saw such an expression of love today? It is well worth our time to talk with God about this. He wants to see "over the top" emotion poured out to Him as Mary unashamedly demonstrated.

The opposite of extravagant is conserving, economical, frugal, penny-pinching, scrimping, skimping, and thrifty. This is the antithesis of God's nature.

What leads us to extravagant action toward God? Our hearts must change. Our part is to create a lifestyle that facilitates this change. We need to forgive others and ourselves. We are to abide in God's Word. Be quick to repent when God shows you something wrong in your heart. Be sold out to go the distance with God. Obey what He tells you to do. Spend time alone with Him in a place set apart in your heart.

The practice of abiding in God will enable you to endure anything. When we abide, we stay in a place, state, or in an attitude of expectancy. We remain, dwell, and continue in Him.

God showed me a beautiful white stone pathway in a dream. As I looked down, I saw "Timothy" written on one of the stones. In the book of 2 Timothy, the theme is to persevere in the gospel despite suffering. I saw the need to press through, set aside time to be with God, pray, wait, ask, and journal. The time I give to God is very precious to Him, and it is never wasted.

We need endurance, lasting power, longevity, and determination in this life. To live in the place of deep endurance comes from having relationship with God and being empowered by his Holy Spirit.

Take your share of suffering for the Message
along with the rest of us. We can only keep on

going, after all, by the power of God Who first saved us and then called us to this holy work. We had nothing to do with it. It was all His idea, a gift prepared for us in Jesus long before we knew anything about it. But we know it now. Since the appearance of our Savior, nothing could be plainer; death defeated, life vindicated in a steady blaze of light, all through the work of Jesus. (2 Timothy 1:8–10 MSG)

# CHAPTER 10

# What about the Trauma?

You can begin to be healed by saying, "I am healed
by the shed blood of the Lord Jesus Christ."

—God

Kelsi suffered from both emotional and spiritual injury most of
her life. John and I experienced the secondary damage of feeling
her trials for many years. We also reeled under the full brunt of the
trauma of the ending of her life here. We are not alone in having to
deal with this monster. Others I know have lost children and have
dealt with losses of many different kinds.

Trauma is a huge issue in our world today.

Trauma is an emotional response to a terri-
ble event like an accident, rape or natural disas-
ter. Immediately after the event, shock and denial
are typical. Longer term reactions include unpre-
dictable emotions, flashbacks, strained relationships and even physical symptoms like headaches
or nausea. While these feelings are normal, some
people have difficulty moving on with their lives.

Psychologists can help these individuals find constructive ways of managing their emotions.[23]

Talk therapy combined with methods such as EMDR (eye movement desensitization and reprocessing) and even EFT (emotional freedom techniques) such as tapping on certain parts of the body while saying calming statements may be used in the therapeutic process to overcome or at least greatly mute the voice of trauma. Some medications are also a useful adjunctive measure. There is evidence in the literature that supports these methods.

In Christian counseling, prayer to God as Father, Son Jesus Christ, and the Holy Spirit is often employed. Andrew Miller developed his approach to healing called "HeartSync." He explains in detail about different parts of the whole that make up each person. Trauma fragments personality into separate compartments where emotions are held. Some of these soul fragments are younger essences of the whole personality. Other pieces that emerge in counseling may feel to be of any age. The idea of fragmentation is not new even in the secular literature. For example, Janina Fisher, PhD, is a psychotherapist with extensive training in trauma and dissociation. One of her books is entitled *Healing the Fragmented Selves of Trauma Survivors: Overcoming Internal Self-Alienation.*

Internal conflict develops from self-alienation. It is necessary to recognize the disagreements about self that arise due to trauma. Self-blame is a big part of the picture. Common statements heard in therapy include "what did I do wrong" or "I am a loser" when the person did nothing to bring on the trauma. If a parent was the oppressor, the child would both want to run to the parent and away from them but not blame them because that would be too overwhelming. The child must still live with that parent and would have to develop separate "selves" and coping strategies to survive. It is important to note that our brains of necessity allow fragmentation to occur in order to live

---

23 "Trauma," American Psychological Assn, www.apa.org/topics/trauma#:~:text= Trauma%20is%20an%20emotional%20response,symptoms%20like%20 headaches%20or%20nause.

through intolerable trauma. When that child becomes an adult, it is necessary to begin the healing process of restoring wholeness to the personality.

Pastor Patti Valotta has written *A Practicum-Immanuel*, which explains her approach to the healing of trauma. During an initial prayer time, all evil is evicted from the room except anything that the Lord Jesus allows to remain in order for His healing purposes to manifest. Sometimes one needs to know what particular evil has accosted them before it is overcome. It is notable that the therapist acts only as a "coach" who is also listening to God in prayer. During the initial prayer time, the person then asks God to help them remember a time when they felt very connected to Him. The coach helps the person express thanks for the memory where they aligned in peace with Jesus because expressing gratitude to God opens up one's relational circuits in the brain. (This is also covered in Dr. Karl Lehman's book *Outsmarting Yourself*, which was previously cited.) The next step is to connect with Jesus in the present before asking what He wants the person to know that day. Sometimes a memory appears, and the coach directs them to look for Jesus in that traumatic memory. Should the person find Him, Jesus does something very healing within the trauma, and the person is changed. If Jesus is not found, the person is redirected back to the present where they are able to reexperience the Lord's presence with them. Often, God is building capacity in relationship in this back-and-forth time until His loved one is ready to "go there" and see Him acting on their behalf in the past.

This is a very safe process. The Word says, "You have beset me and shut me in—behind and before, and You have laid Your hand upon me" (Psalm 139:5 AMP). In other words, God is in your past, protecting you from it, He is in your present, and He is also ahead, in your future all at the same time. One must go through some pain in retrieved memories, but when Jesus is seen in them, a supernatural healing occurs.

There is no cookie-cutter formula to follow in dealing with trauma. Loving the person and listening to them is healing in itself. A Christian therapist may utilize EMDR, EFT, HeartSync, the

Immanuel approach, or any other heart-connecting way God reveals. There is something else that heals trauma, which I will explain by a story.

I took a trip to Scotland and Ireland several years ago. The excursion was headed by Kathie Walters, a well-known seer. Amazing supernatural events occurred, but what stood out to me the most was how God corrected me and changed my heart toward a young man there.

The bus driver played various CDs of beautiful Celtic music as we traveled to our destinations. This young man could not contain himself. He would jump out of his seat, full of energy. It so "happened" that he came right next to my seat when he would kick up his heels and dance! He laughed and carried on until the music stopped. I thought he might hit my face, and I was quite disconcerted. What was going on with him? I wondered.

One day, he came on the bus dressed in a long white robe. This was definitely different! A husband and wife accompanied him. They protected him in prayer. Many of us went into the town of Galway to see the sights. He and his two companions went elsewhere. When we gathered together at the end of the day, I asked them where they had gone. The wife told me what happened. The husband admitted he was very uncomfortable until he saw what God did.

"We went to a nearby park and saw a homeless man. He had just tried to kill himself, but medics were called. They found him and bandaged him up. He just sat there, totally dejected, hopeless, slumped over. Our friend began to dance before him. There were some teenagers nearby, and they began to mock the three of us as my husband and I stood by to protect and honor the dance. The jeers got louder, but he just kept dancing. He didn't even seem to hear them. Within a few minutes, the homeless man raised his head, and tears began to stream from his eyes. All the catcalls abruptly stopped. Something happened. We know he received a healing from God. When our friend stopped dancing, we blessed him and went on our way," the wife finished.

I was humbled as I listened. Would I ever yield to the Holy Spirit in such a way? At the end of our trip, I had occasion to talk with this young man. The wife of the couple told me he had had a very traumatic upbringing. Now I knew what I was seeing was the impact of God on one life. So I asked him a question.

"Your friend told me you suffered a lot of trauma in your life. One would never know it, to see you now. How did you get so healed from it?"

He looked at me with honesty and deep love. His answer was simple and direct and not given in a full sentence.

"Hours and hours in His presence," he said.

Ah, worship of Jesus heals trauma. That is very good to know. It made sense to me because one cannot spend a great deal of time with God without being transformed.

I believe it takes very little to traumatize us. We come from our Source, God, Who is all loving and all knowing. We were made out of love, to receive and to give love back. God is the Father of all our spirits. He sends our spirit forth from His Presence and knits it together with our soul in our mother's womb. It is a mystery. The good news is, God had us first. He knows what we will confront when we enter this dimension. He puts what we need into our spirits, and we may unpack this into our souls as we mature. This is good news.

Once God places us in the womb, there may be generational spirits of iniquity that have access to us. If repeated, where sins come down the bloodline and nobody repented of them, there is an open door of attack against us. This is something that may be uncovered during prayer. Generational identificational repentance will lift the burden of evil from the person. In such a prayer, we identify with the sins of our ancestors. We repent and renounce them before God. We ask God to cleanse the generational line by the Blood of Jesus to the present generation and forward over our children, grandchildren and until Jesus returns. We forgive ancestors and self for the iniquities. The result is a tangible shift of healing.

As stated previously, repentance is necessary in order to grow in holiness. When God grants repentance to us, it is life-changing.

> For godly grief and the pain God is permit-
> ted to direct, produce a repentance that leads and

> contributes to salvation and deliverance from evil, and it never brings regret; but worldly grief (the hopeless sorrow that is characteristic of the pagan world) is deadly (breeding and ending in death). (2 Corinthians 7:10)

Trauma may be acute, chronic, or complex. There are different symptoms associated with these three types. Kelsi's was chronic and complex. Unfortunately, in today's world, most people experience more than one single intolerable event in their lifetime.

My online *Webster's* dictionary app defines *trauma* as "a disordered psychic or behavioral state resulting from severe mental or emotional stress or physical injury; an emotional upset." The history of the word comes from the Greek "traumat," meaning a wound, and it is akin to another Greek word that means to pierce. From the same source, the word "pierce" means to stab, to enter or thrust into sharply or painfully, to penetrate with the eye or mind, or to discern (separate mentally one thing from another), or to penetrate so as to move or touch the emotions of.

Of all the definitions, "pierce" described our experience the best. Kelsi moving to heaven thrust sharply through each beat of our hearts to a degree I cannot adequately describe. Stabbing pain accompanied most of our steps for the first four months. Neither John nor I ever felt anything as awful or deep. Our emotions were stuck on great loss, loneliness, and the ache of her absence. Eventually I considered Another Who was pierced.

> But He was pierced because of our transgressions, crushed because of our iniquities; punishment for our peace was on Him, and we are healed by His wounds. (Isaiah 53:5 HCSB)

Jesus took on every trauma that was ever experienced by human beings. He became sin for us on the cross. He died and was buried. He was resurrected on the third day and overcame everything He took on to set us free. When we accept Him into our hearts as Savior, we exchange our sin for His righteousness. The Holy Spirit gave me an amazing key one night as I was crying without ceasing and longing for Kelsi.

"Listen, you can begin to be healed by saying, 'I am healed by the shed blood of the Lord Jesus Christ,'" He said.

He broke through my heaving sobs with a direct and gentle tone. It worked. I began to say this as I took daily communion with Him. I did it in faith. It took time and effort on my part to agree with Him. It was better than the daily death spiral when I listened to my own mind, will, and emotions. God interrupted my trauma, and I decided to follow His counsel.

When I asked God how it was possible for me to find stability so quickly even during the first few months, His answer was simple.

"Because you chose," He said. I knew He meant I chose to listen to Him no matter how my feelings swirled inside. I chose joy. I said it out loud every day.

I did not join a grief group or see a professional counselor, although it can be very helpful to do so. I received much help from my friends whose children had "gone ahead" of them. It is very life-saving to talk to another person who has suffered a similar loss and come through it because it gives hope that you will survive. I prayed, heard God, and obeyed. I pressed in and continued to ponder Him and His ways. The Holy Spirit was my best counselor. It is one of His names. Jesus explained Him this way.

> However, I am telling you nothing but the truth when I say it is profitable (good, expedient, advantageous) for you that I go away. Because if I do not go away, the Comforter (Counselor, Helper, Advocate, Intercessor, Strengthener, Standby) will not come to you (into close fellowship with you: but if I go away, I will send Him to you (to be in close fellowship with you). (John 16:7 AMP)

God spoke things to me that could offend others in their grief. Could you imagine a human being telling a grieving parent that "grief consumes, just keep your eyes on Jesus"? Our humanistic response is to say that grief is a process that can take from one to two years or longer if it is complex grief. No friend or counselor would say, "Listen, it's a joy to serve Jesus!" a few months in to such a dark place. Would you expect to hear that heaven is celebrating the return of your loved one and perhaps you could also see it that way? We do not say these things to others who go through this. I am not suggesting that we do. Yet God said these things to me. The truth is, He saved my emotional life. He gave me hope. Several months after Kelsi was gone, I listened to another mother who lost her only child. She spoke about her relationship with the Holy Spirit, and she said those same words, that He saved her life.

God told me how delighted He was to have Kelsi there with Him in the celestial realm. He showed her to my sister as completely healed. He spoke life back into my husband. We all experienced joy and peace after our encounters with God. He spoke the word "martyrs" to me as I read the Bible. Later I surmised He meant Kelsi was a martyr for His kingdom. I believe that carries a significant weight of glory for Jesus.

According to my online *Merriam-Webster* dictionary, the closest definition for *martyr* that pertained to Kelsi would be under "victim, especially a great or constant sufferer." Some people who read my first memoir said they didn't realize the extent of her anguish. This word comes from the Greek word *martys*, which means witness.

The first definition for *witness* is "attestation of a fact or event; testimony." Another meaning is "something serving as evidence or proof: sign." Also, "public affirmation by word or example of usually religious faith or conviction." Kelsi was all of this. Her testimony was her great love for God no matter what she went through. The words of wisdom that came forth from her at times took my breath away. She was a supernatural sign from God. She often told me when I was "off" about the Lord. She affirmed her faith all the time in public. One time when we were at her psychiatrist's office, she talked out loud about angels, and I advised her to talk more quietly.

"I don't care if they hear me, Mom," she said. I was convicted again.

There is an unseen realm. Creation as we see it came from that realm where God resides. I advise you to read Phil Mason's *Quantum Glory: The Science of Heaven Invading Earth*. Mr. Mason describes in easy-to-understand detail how the quirky world of quantum physics works. Quantum means it is too small to be seen with the naked eye. He ties in the mind-blowing scientific findings with the Bible in a masterful way. My faith increased after reading his book.

My rational mind struggled to accept God's perspective. However, I noted that the tsunami waves quieted to a gentle rhythmic roll inside every time I heard His voice. Kelsi heard Him more clearly than I did. Her raging reactions simply stopped when He spoke. My first memoir details many of these conversations. It was always a miracle.

> He hushes the storm to a calm and to a gentle whisper, so that the waves of the sea are still.
> (PSALM 107:29 AMP)

Because I have been through the worst traumatic experience of my life, I can assure you of one thing. God does speak today. He cares about everything we go through. He is supremely high above us, His creation, yet He enters our lives gently and lovingly. He provides healing in frankly amazing ways. We are able to connect with Him, not through our intellect but through our heart. We can hear from and speak to our Creator! It is all thanks to the sacrifice of Jesus on the cross, which brought us into relationship with the Father. We now have access "beyond the veil" into direct contact with our God.

Take note, the word "pierce" also means to discern. This means we are able to separate out one thing from another. We can identify something as distinct from something else. We can apprehend, decipher, and decode problems. This leads me to believe that when we are pierced, when we go through trauma, there is an actual benefit embedded within. It may greatly increase our discernment of things in both the seen and unseen realms. This is what has happened in my own life. By God's grace and mercy, I have come through this great trauma to the other side. I did not see how that was possible. God made the way. I now testify about it and show forth His glory in it.

God heals trauma. It happens when we connect with His Presence through worship. It occurs through counselors using any of a number of techniques. As we pray, He speaks directly into our hearts, and we are transformed. Most of my healing came from hearing His voice, receiving the support of Denise, Beverly, and my family and also through worship.

> The sheep that are My own hear and are listening to My voice; and I know them, and they follow Me. (John 10:27 AMP)

Amen.

# CHAPTER 11

# Have Faith in God

I believe in Christianity as I believe that the sun has risen: not only because I see it, but because by it I see everything else.

—C. S. Lewis

The day after Kelsi moved to heaven, I asked God what He expected of me now. I was shattered and disoriented from the trauma and grief, but I also had relationship with Him. He had been drawing me to Himself for years. I knew Jesus as my Savior, Friend, Redeemer, Counselor, Advocate, and Life Source. I turned to Him in my darkest hour, and He answered.

"An honest life contribution," He said. I understood this was for the purpose of helping others. Maybe you would not expect God to say this to me at that point in time. But He did. As always, I recorded His words because every time He spoke, He rescued me. No matter what we face in terms of pain, loss, or horror, He is fully able to restore us. He does this because He loves us so deeply. We have infinite worth in His eyes. As we respond to His healing, we are rejuvenated, brought back to life but in a deeper, richer sense. We change the lives of people who come into contact with us in ways that could only come because of what we have lived through. It's true.

"I'm a Constant," He also told me. That word means He is marked by firm steadfast resolution or faithfulness. God is invariable in this. He is perpetually flowing above, around, and in us. We can choose to be distracted by worldly things and thus stifle Him. We also have the power to fix our minds on Him. We may commune with our Creator. When we try to maintain some type of status quo in life, it is due to the deception that we have control.

When we move toward relationship with God, when we lean in to truly listen, He says amazing things. Though we do have trouble in this world, He provides shelter.

God sheltered Kelsi many times throughout her life, but her body did not survive. My relationship with God drove me to seek Him on this. I realized that God moved in all her decisions that day to bring her home to Himself. She is now fully functioning in the mind of Christ because she is in heaven with Him. We have the mind of Christ here, but imperfectly as we live in a fallen state. She had suffered long enough while she was here. All our times are in God's hands. I believe it was Kelsi's time to go home to heaven despite all the error and fallenness around how she exited.

When we choose to commune or communicate intimately with the Lord, we relate to and bond with Him. We learn to love. We see others with brand-new eyes. Instead of noticing their faults, we see their potential. We grow in love, joy, peace, patience, kindness, goodness, gentleness, faithfulness, and self-control as we continue to be transformed into the image of Jesus. Consider how amazing God truly is.

> Before anything else existed, God was. The idea that something or someone exists outside of time is mind-boggling. Still, it is a logical necessity that something had to come first, and that first something had to always exist. The Bible's answer to this mystery is straight-forward: "Before the mountains were created, before you made the earth... You are God, without beginning or end."[24]

---

[24] "Isaiah," NLT Bible: New Living Translation (Tyndale House Publishers, Inc, 1992), 656–656.

The above excerpt is taken from an explanatory page in Kelsi's Student's Life Application Bible. It explains God has characteristics that are either incommunicable (those He does not share with us) and communicable (those He does reveal). We are able to understand God's communicable attributes and share, to some degree, in His ability to think, love, work, and make moral judgments. His existence, immutability, and infinity are those characteristics we do not share with Him, but we accept them in faith. He gives all of us a measure of faith to receive this.

I remember the day Kelsi told me she asked God this question. "Well, who created You, God?" she said she heard Him chuckle.

"I'm not going to tell you everything. Just believe I always was," He said. So she did.

What is faith and why do we need it? The Bible answers this question.

What is faith? It is the confident assurance that what we hope for is going to happen. It is the evidence of things we cannot yet see. God gave His approval to people in days of old because of their faith. By faith we understand that the entire universe was formed at God's command, that what we now see did not come from anything that can be seen. It was by faith that Abel brought a more acceptable offering to God than Cain did. God accepted Abel's offering to show that he was a righteous man. And although Abel is long dead, he still speaks to us because of his faith. It was by faith that Enoch was taken up to heaven without dying—suddenly he disappeared because God took him. But before he was taken up, he was approved as pleasing to God. So, you see, it is impossible to please God without faith. Anyone who wants to come to Him must believe that there is a God and that He rewards those who sincerely seek Him. (Hebrews 11: 1–6 NLT)

What we see did not come from anything that can be seen. Do we understand this statement? I previously made reference to Phil Mason's book *Quantum Glory*. The subtitle is *The Science of Heaven Invading Earth*. For deeper understanding, you will need to read his book. I will highlight a few of the most important findings because it will increase your faith as it has mine.

Quantum systems include photons and electrons, things smaller than an atom. These particles can be in more than one state (either a wave or a particle) and one specific location at any time. It is hypothesized that they are in every state at the same time until someone observes them. If one expects to see them as a wave, that's how they show up. If one intends to see them as a particle, voilà, that is how they appear. The observer effect cannot be separated from their actual state at any moment.

Through precise and replicated experiments, subatomic particles have been proven to be nonlocal. This means they are nonmaterial and "outside of the time-space manifold." Space is three dimensional, and ever since Einstein, time is understood to constitute the fourth dimension. But the nonlocal realities of the quantum world point to the existence of yet another dimension of reality that is not bound by either locality or by time. Scientists appear to have stumbled upon empirical evidence for the existence of additional dimensions! This ought to be headline news around the world![25]

In our realm, there is cause and effect. If a large ship passes nearby your canoe, you will feel the effect of the waves against it. That means it is "local" because you can identify where it comes from. This is not how the quantum world operates.

Quantum entanglement shows that once particles become entangled, they retain a powerful connection even if they are then separated by great distances. Brian Clegg, a secular author, called this "the God effect" and said it has an "unsettling omnipresence."[26] Such

[25] Phil Mason, *Quantum Glory: The Science of Heaven Invading Earth* (SOS Print and Media Group, 2012).

[26] Ibid.

particles, once disentangled, communicate instantaneously over vast distances.

Quantum tunneling is another mystery. Experiments have shown that matter has the capacity to dematerialize and to rematerialize in the subatomic world. If such a particle encounters a barrier and does not have the energy to get over it, there is a probability it can tunnel through it.

Quantum teleportation has been demonstrated by Austrian researchers who teleported photons of light across the Danube River in Vienna. They dematerialized the photons and transferred their configuration to another location where they were then reconstructed. Science is showing a microscopic world just as real as what we see with our eyes. These new discoveries in the unseen realm undergird our observable realm.

Mr. Mason states his thesis as this,

> God created this physical world as a physical materialization of non-local components and He sustains this materialization of the wave function with His powerful voice. The material world is structured upon the building blocks of spirit.[27]

He also proposes that the invisible layer of quantum reality may be an interface between the presence and power of God, Who is Spirit, and our world of matter.

I know there are two worlds. They are the world of matter and the world of Spirit. Jesus spoke of this,

> My kingdom is not from here (this world): (it has no such origin or source). (John 18:36 AMP)

---

[27] Ibid.

The writer of Hebrews tells us,

> (But) in the last of these days He has spoken to us in (the person of a) Son, Whom He appointed Heir and lawful Owner of all things, also by and through Whom He created the worlds and the reaches of space and the ages of time (He made, produced, built, operated and arranged them in order). (Hebrews 1:2 AMP)

The word "worlds" is plural here.

> Through faith we understand that the worlds were framed by the word of God, so that things which are seen were not made of things which do appear. (Hebrews 11:3 KJV)

Everything we can observe came from the unseen realm. You sit on a chair that is in reality constructed of subatomic particles of light. At the core of our physical being, we humans are also constructed from the light that comes from God, Who is Spirit.

Several years ago, God gave me a powerful dream that connects some of these realities now. I did not understand at that time how quantum physics would answer one part of this dream. I was walking up a ramp toward a wall that had beautifully colored flowers on it. I knew that I could pass through that wall somehow. Instead I walked into a room where there was a very tall being. He informed me that "It's time to leave your passport here," as he thumped the table for emphasis. Perhaps a year later, I understood God was telling me that He loved me much more than I understood. I heard a preacher say, "You are much more than having your passport stamped to get to heaven, beloved." I did not see the deeper implications of walking through the wall until I read Mr. Mason's book and then remembered what Jesus did.

In Luke 4, it is recorded how Jesus overcame all the temptations of the devil. At the end of the forty days, Jesus returned in the power of the Spirit and began teaching in the synagogues. He was rejected in Nazareth because they knew Him from childhood. He responded that a prophet is not accepted in his own country. Then He reminded them that, instead of Jews, there were Gentiles who were saved and healed of disease in the past by the prophets Elijah and Elisha. The Jews in Nazareth became so incensed that they attempted to kill Him.

> And all they in the synagogue, when they heard these things, were filled with wrath. And rose up, and thrust Him out of the city, and led Him unto the brow of the hill whereon their city was built, that they might cast Him down head-long (over the cliff). But He passing through the midst of them went His way. (Luke 4:28–30 KJV)

We pass over these statements in the Bible too easily. How did that actually happen? They had their hands on Him. Many of them had hold as they pushed Him up the hill to cast Him over. They were full of murderous intent and would not have let go of Him. Yet He just "passed through their midst"? What do those words mean?

I use the *New Strong's Expanded Exhaustive Concordance of the Bible*. The Greek word for "passing" is *dierchomai*, and it means to come or go through, to traverse (to move or pass along or through), and it can mean a route or way across or over. "Through" is a function word that indicates movement into one point and out to another point. It indicates the means or agency (force) behind the function. It means going from a point of origin to another destination without changing. "Through" comes from the Latin, which means across or beyond. It also originates from Sanskrit for "he crosses over."

As I put the world of quantum physics next to the Bible, I see that Jesus simply dematerialized within the midst of this raging crowd. Remember, there had to be at least several strong and angry full-grown men who had hold of Him. He could not break free in the natural. God rematerialized Him elsewhere. It does not tell us where He ended up. Verse 30 simply explains that He then "went His way."

It was not yet Jesus's time to be killed, so man could not do it. I believe Jesus crossed over from the origin of Nazareth to another point on the earth through the power of God utilizing the mechanics of quantum physics.

This was not the only time in the Bible that a man disappeared. Philip, one of the original apostles, was told by God to go meet an Ethiopian eunuch who was sitting in his chariot on the road to Gaza. He was reading chapter 53 in the book of Isaiah, which described Jesus, but he had not heard of Him. Philip found him. They began to ride in his chariot together as Philip explained that Jesus was the suffering servant in that passage. As they came to some water, Philip baptized the official.

> And when they came up out of the water, the Spirit of the Lord (suddenly) caught away Philip; and the eunuch saw him no more, and he went on his way rejoicing. (Acts 8:39 AMP)

It sounds to me like God dematerialized Philip and placed him elsewhere on the earth, as He had done with His Son previously.

Mr. Mason quotes Jean Staune, a French professor of philosophy. He wrote an essay called "On the Edge of Physics."

> Quantum physics does not prove the existence of God. It nonetheless takes us through a giant step from a scientific materialism that ruled out the existence of God, to a position where, on a scientific basis, we can start to understand the concept of God's existence. A belief in materialism is still possible under quantum physics, of course—but only if it is transformed into a kind of "science fiction" materialism, somehow able to integrate the "de-materialization of matter." New experiments show that matter itself does not have a strictly material reality.[28]

---

[28] Ibid.

I was at a writer's conference in Texas. In the morning, I had a sudden thought to read about quantum physics. I knew I had down-loaded Mr. Mason's book onto my kindle but had not yet read it. I started it that morning. When I got to the conference, out of the blue, one of the attendees told me I should read another book, which was also about quantum physics. This was a witness to what God said to me. He will always underscore what He tells you to do. All of this may be too quirky or threatening for some to understand. I am not saying you have to believe it. I am just giving my honest life's contribution in telling you my story of how God speaks to me. I do believe the evidence from quantum physics is so compelling it is causing scientists to turn to God. They can no longer ignore or push Him out of the equation of creation. He is the Equation, and He wants us to know that.

I hope this increases your hunger to read about the quantum world. Go to Father God and talk with Him about it. It always increases my faith to follow God's promptings. It also gives me great delight to increase in understanding of anything about Him.

There will always be more to learn about our Lord Jesus, even in eternity. That is a very exciting truth.

I decided to just trust God many years ago. This choice was not predicated on how well our lives were going at that time. It was made in spite of it. I trust God more today than I did then. This is only explainable because of His love, His magnificence, and His constant faithfulness that He has communicated to me through all the diffi-cult circumstances of my life. He has supernaturally healed me of so much trauma I can only bow to my knees before Him. He is my Anchor, my constant and abiding Hope and Teacher, and my Friend.

I love You, Lord Jesus.

# CHAPTER 12

# Persistent Love, Obedient Words

Make it a goal to sparkle every day.

—Kathi Basehore

I have read that when you write a book, you should have the end in mind. I know people often prepare outlines and even know what each chapter will cover. It has not worked that way for me. I start to write, and the contents for the next chapter emerge after I have spent time in God's presence. It was the same with my first book. I was so surprised at how it all came together for each individual chapter and then for the book as a whole.

God told me this book was "already written in heaven." It was a faith walk to start the process a second time. I was afraid to write, not wanting to reexperience the pain and trauma of those first months after Kelsi departed. I knew God wanted me to write about this journey, but I balked more this time.

I took three weeks off to write. I stopped for five days during that time. My friend Marie is one of two people who pray for me on a regular basis. In an email, she said she was asking God about me, and suddenly, she saw a book in front of her, and it was vibrating. She felt like the word *book* was being shouted at her as it shook in the vision. I sheepishly admitted I had not been writing. I got back up on the horse the next day. The content for the chapters began to flow for the rest of the designated time. I also thank Debby who prays and tells me what God says to her. This is why we need each other. God will give things to others for our benefit. He will reveal things to us for theirs. I am also very grateful to the people in our church prayer group for their spiritual interventions on behalf of our local church body. If we are not praying, the enemy is advancing. When we pray for each other, we "lock shields" like the ancient Roman soldiers did so they could move forward on the battlefield. We conquer together as we do so.

When the flow of writing stopped for the day, I sought God, and He uncorked the next chapter. I wanted this book to be as fresh and full of Him as possible. He directed me to write about the power of words in this chapter. Words spoken by us, about us, or to us either take us toward our destiny or away from it.

Death and life are in the power of the tongue, and they who indulge in it shall eat the fruit of it (for death or life). (Proverbs 18:21 AMP)

You offspring of vipers! How can you speak good things when you are evil? For out of the full- ness (the overflow, the superabundance) of the heart the mouth speaks. The good man from his inner good treasure flings forth good things, and the evil man out of his inner evil storehouse flings forth evil things. But I tell you, on the day of judg- ment men will have to give account for every idle (inoperative, nonworking) word they speak. For by your words you will be justified and acquitted, and by your words you will be condemned and sentenced. (Matthew 12:34–37 AMP)

I do not want to be condemned and sentenced by idle words when I stand before the Lord. Repent when you spew words of gos- sip, accusation, or judgment.

I can sense the heaviness of negative words whether I speak them or someone else speaks critically. Such words promote actual failure or a failure mentality. When spoken by authority figures in childhood, the wounds cut to the deepest degree. Children, being egocentric, take on blame for abusive words. They cannot blame the adult from whom the verbiage spills especially if that adult is a parent or older person with whom they reside. Self-blame becomes the temporary yet fairly effective fix to the trauma of abuse. It must be based in lies about the self, so this will result in damage, which will become apparent to others via relationship difficulties or will remain hidden behind a façade. A person may appear highly functioning while harboring deep unconscious pain attached to painful beliefs about the self.

Children grow to adulthood, unaware of the malicious subconscious chatter, of the buried deceit that pummels. Here are a few common examples of inner lies, beliefs, and then truth, which refutes them.

| The Lie | The Belief | The Truth |
| --- | --- | --- |
| You don't have what it takes | I'm a loser | I'm gifted to overcome |
| You should be ashamed | I am bad | I am made in God's Image |
| You can't do that | I am incapable | I can do it |
| You're not smart enough | I am stupid | I am intelligent |

When people begin to uncover the lies, I explain such thoughts do not emanate from our good God.

> How precious and weighty also are Your thoughts to me, O God! How vast is the sum of them! If I could count them, they would be more in number than the sand. (Psalm 139:17–18 AMP)

God constantly thinks good thoughts about us. The source for evil thoughts and condemnation is evil spirits in the unseen realm. I know this because I have heard them. One time, I heard a spirit suggest that I should probably kill myself. I told it to get out of my house. About one hour later, Kelsi came to me in great distress, stating she felt so badly she thought she should kill herself. Immediately I discerned the same spirit and explained how she should take authority over it. She did and was totally fine thereafter.

Another time, a spirit spoke to me in a long paragraph of derisive words about my character, ending with "you are such a loser." I knew this was not me thinking inside my own head. The vitriol behind the words convinced me that the enemy desired to kill me. Others may not hear into the spirit realm very clearly. Think of it this way. The Word of God tells us how God speaks. He may chastise, but His arm envelops as He explains how to get back on the correct path. The source of hatred behind words that mean to destroy must therefore come from another spiritual source.

The good news is, no matter how many lies one absorbed as a child, God is fully capable of leading us out of bondage into truth and freedom. He may do it through other loving people who come into our lives or He may speak truth directly into our being. He wants us to pray for each other about this.

It takes time and effort to uncover inner deception, but it is well worth it. Once exposed, you can set it out before you and say, "I see you now. I believe I am incapable, but the truth is, I can do this thing. In fact, God has called me to do it. I will no longer be held in captivity to you. I will move forward and set the necessary goals to achieve the task. God is for me and will enable me to accomplish this."

It is necessary to confront the lies, but it takes the power and presence of Almighty God to fully break their influence in our lives. That is why I seek His presence so much.

One of the lies shame told me was that I was not to be seen.

Too late, shame. God told me I would write a bunch of books, and this is number two.

> You keep track of all my sorrows. You have collected all my tears in your bottle. You have recorded each one in your book. (Psalm 56:8 NLT)

This is what God does with our tears. He does not let one moment of pain go unnoticed. We may travail with agony, but I know that joy comes because the Joyful One is in me.

> For His anger is but for a moment but
> His favor is for a lifetime or in His favor is life.
> Weeping may endure for a night, but joy comes
> in the morning. (Psalm 30:5 AMP)

The Word says that what we suffer produces a glory in us as we continue to look toward Jesus.

> For our light, momentary afflictions is ever
> more and more abundantly preparing and pro-
> ducing and achieving for us an everlasting weight
> of glory (beyond all measure, excessively surpass-
> ing all comparisons and all calculations, a vast
> and transcendent glory and blessedness never
> to cease!) Since we consider and look not to the
> things that are seen but to the things that are
> unseen: for the things that are visible are temporal
> (brief and fleeting) but the things that are invis-
> ible are deathless and everlasting. (2 Corinthians
> 4:17–18 AMP)

My emotions about Kelsi moving to heaven nearly crushed me. God brought me out of death to life as He reminded me to keep my eyes on Him. I held onto His life raft. Moment by moment, I chose to focus on Jesus. The result of such communion has resulted in His desire becoming mine. I desire to pour into the lives of others in love for the remainder of my time here.

God knows us intimately. He will comfort us in the individual way each one of us needs. How He has spoken to me is how He has healed me. He may speak very differently to you because you are unique, beau-tifully crafted and designed with grace, intelligence, and care. You are precious, and He will touch you with precision, mercy, and love.

As Kelsi persisted, so do I. I choose to go on resolutely in spite of opposition. I endure, hold on, and keep it up. I refuse to desist, discontinue, or quit because I will not agree with my enemy who wants to shut me up. God expects me to continue, so I move forward. He actually told me I would not fail in my heart toward Him. The confidence in His voice when He said that lit a fire in me to finish this task in spite of the fear to reexperience great pain. In the same way, our words inspire either hope or despair. They create sparkles within others or deflate them.

Negative words do create discouragement. They frustrate others and hinder their advancement in life. It is quite difficult to have relationship with someone who has an "Eyor" mindset. Dr. Caroline Leaf has cited research showing that negative thoughts grow brown-stunted proteins in the brain. An accumulation of these calls forth the image of a thorn forest. Positive thoughts result in the formation of a nicely formed green protein, which, when multiplied, resemble a beautiful green tree. When faithless words are spoken, destroy their effect by stating God's words of hope and truth. The Word of God shifts the atmosphere over people and creates brains full of trees of life.

For example, one may complain that "everything is falling apart." Perhaps multiple events transpired, which incurred financial strain. Reframe such words by empathizing with the current upheaval and then give assurance that the ordeal will be overcome. Bring to mind what Jesus said in Matthew 6:25–31. Worry is a pointless mind exercise. As God clothes the grass of the field, we may pray, put our faith forward, and expect that He will care for us. God often arranges real needs to be met through human means. I always see faces change with hope as they pull back from their own pessimistic expectations. This is exciting, to realize that we may encourage and so inspire each other with courage, spirit, and hope. We have the power to spur people on, to stimulate them toward their destinies.

I will never forget the time a woman said I gave hope to her. I was setting up my chair and table to start that day's session, and I absentmindedly said that was a good thing. She corrected me.

"It was EVERYTHING," she said. Startled, I looked into her eyes and felt the weight of her gratitude.

"I'm sorry, you are so welcome. It was an honor to help," I said. My words brought her out of hopelessness. We cannot put a price on the effect of our words. They truly are life or death to others.

> Death and life are in the power of the tongue,
> and they who indulge in it shall eat the fruit of it
> (for death or life). (Proverbs 18:21 AMP)

Make it a goal to sparkle every day. Pour out from the Holy Spirit's river of life inside onto those around you. We reflect the luminescence of God as we do so. In fact, one of the definitions of sparkle is "to perform brilliantly." We cause others to "glitter or shine" with life. Our speech is to burn with holy fire and so ignite humanity with confident vision for their future.

I prophesy into you now as you read this book. God is bringing you into a whole new adventure. The things that have come against you in the past are now breaking down before you. New light and clarity are coming into your vision as you participate with God's plan. You shall sparkle with a new incandescence that will illuminate not only your own path, but the paths of others around you. Yours is a glorious future in Jesus Christ. His provision will fulfill the vision He has for you.

We all have a story to tell. You may not write a book about yours, but you will be called upon to share your testimony in some way with humanity. Do not be afraid to do this. It will change lives. I have seen this happen when I speak life into others, and I have received understanding of how these written words are moving upon those who read them. Either way, it is wisdom to write down the goals you receive from heaven. I put a stake into the ground with my first book, and the earth shook. Not because it was *number one on Amazon*, but due to my obedience to my King.

> Then the Lord replied: Write down the revelation and make it plain on tablets so that a herald may run with it. (Habakkuk 2:2)

Run with this one, Lord. Amen.

# CHAPTER 13

# Focus on Scripture Brings Joy

The direction of your focus is the direction
your life will move. Let yourself move toward
what is good, valuable, strong and true.

—Ralph Marston

One of the main weapons Satan uses is distraction. A distraction is anything that removes our focus away from God and the task at hand. Focus involves being able to concentrate. When we do so, we are directing our attention with intent toward an activity. We receive power when we focus on Jesus and His Word. Our busy brains calm down. The Scriptures also bring healing to our bodies.

My son, attend to my words; consent and
submit to my sayings. Let them not depart from
your sight; keep them in the center of your heart.
For they are life to those who find them, healing
and health to all their flesh. (Proverbs 4:20–22
AMP)

Find a quiet place, close the door, and turn off your cell phone. Inform your family you are unavailable for some time. When pressured thoughts arise, discharge them by writing them down or dictating them. Use the voice recorder on your cell phone or a small Dictaphone. I will give examples of how to pray the Scriptures back to God.

Jesus tells us that He is the Way, the Truth, and the Life. He emphasizes that no one is able to come to the Father except through Himself. The world lies and says there are many paths to God. It is a great deception that has ensnared many people. Do not fall for this. You will only enter heaven through God's Son, Jesus Christ.

> Enter through the narrow gate; for wide is the gate and spacious and broad is the way that leads away to destruction, and many are those who are entering through it. But the gate is narrow and the way is straitened and compressed that leads away to life, and few are those who find it. (Matthew 7:13–14 AMP)

It's not supposed to be easy here on earth. It is a battle zone. We are in a war. Our God has triumphed over Satan, and we are to mature and believe that. It is our job to believe, not to strive in doing works of the flesh. Out of deep belief, faith, and trust in Jesus, those works that we were sent here to accomplish flow forth. Our works must flow from the Holy Spirit of God within us. Without growing in intimacy with the One True God Who chooses to live inside of us, we can do nothing of lasting spiritual value.

We may pray these truths like this, "I thank you, Father God, that you have made Your Son, the Lord Jesus Christ, to be the only way to come to You. I desire to walk that narrow path You have before me. I trust in Jesus, Your Son, as the Way, Truth, and Life. I believe that Jesus came in the flesh to destroy the works of the devil. I know that He took on all my sin and died in my place. How amazing, Father, that You would do this for me! I desire to do the things You have ordained for me, in partnership with Your Holy Spirit."

Jesus goes on to explain that because we believe in Him, we will do even greater things than He did. He promises that He will grant what we ask in His name so that Father God will be glorified. The key is that God changes our desires to match His. We then pray His heart back to Him, and He grants our prayers.

> (Not in your own strength) for it is God Who is all the while effectually at work in you (energizing and creating in you the power and desire), both to will and to work for His good pleasure and satisfaction and delight. (Philippians 2:13 AMP)

"Father God, I thank You that You are changing my heart's desires to conform to Yours. You are my Source of life. By Your power inside of me, I desire to do those works You have created for me to accomplish before I was born! This brings You great delight as I come to understand my purpose for being here."

If we truly love Jesus, we will obey His commands. We will love others. We will forgive even heinous injustices that have been perpetrated against us. When we do so, we release that person to Jesus. It then becomes an issue between that person and the Lord. When we forgive, it is not just a "good" thing to do that helps us to feel better. We actually release power through our obedience to the Lord, and this changes the lives of others. Forgiveness is not saying that what happened to us was okay or did not matter. It is an act of our will to obey the Lord Jesus Who hung on the cross and became sin for us and Who forgave everyone who murdered Him. Our will is the strongest thing inside of us. Surrender to Jesus comes out of our intimacy with Him. This is where the demons flee.

When Jesus died, we died. When He rose, we rose. He gave it all for us even to shedding His Own Blood. There is no greater love than this.

> No one has greater love than to lay down (give up) his own life for his friends. (John 15:13 AMP)

> Make me go in the path of Your commandments, for in them do I delight. (Psalm 119:35 AMP)

"Lord God, I can never thank You enough for giving me the gift of Your Son, Jesus Christ, Who came in the flesh, lived, died, and rose again for me so that I would have direct access to You, Father God! By Your grace at work in me through Your Holy Spirit, I will love You with all my heart, soul, mind, and strength. I will also love others and even myself, God. I forgive those who have hurt me because You forgave me when You hung on that cross. You actually became sin for me, and even as me. I gladly submit my will to Yours, God. If any part of me struggles with this, would You override it and make me willing to fully surrender my life to You? In this way, You make me go on the path You have chosen for me."

Then the Lord promises that the Father will give us Someone else! There are many names for the Holy Spirit, the third Person of the Trinity. Jesus said that His Holy Spirit represents Himself and acts on His behalf. This Third Person of the Trinity teaches us all things and reminds us of things God has said and is saying.

"Father, thank You so much for sending Your Holy Spirit to live on the inside of me. I know He helps me all the time. He gives me great strength and even prays when I do not know what to pray. I am never alone!"

In the fourteenth chapter of the Gospel of John, Jesus says many comforting things to His disciples. He begins in verse one by encouraging them to not allow their hearts to be agitated. This is something we must do. God will not do this for us. He gives us the way to choose peace. We are to believe and trust in God and His Son.

"Lord, because You said so, I will not let my heart be troubled. I believe in God my Father and in You, Lord Jesus. I ask for Your Presence and peace to fill me up new and fresh right now."

Jesus goes on to say that there are many dwelling places in God's house. He never lied because He never sinned.

> If it were not so, I would have told you; for I am going away to prepare a place for you. And when I go and make ready a place for you, I will come back again and will take you to Myself, that where I am you may be also. (John 14:2–3 AMP)

We who believe in Jesus will have our own home in heaven! There is plenty of space in the spiritual realm. Jesus has declared this.

"Lord, I thank You that I have a home You are preparing for me in heaven. Not only have You gone ahead to prepare it for me, You are also returning to take me to Yourself. How astounding that I will be where You are! I will actually see you face to face and know You as You know me."

Peace is available to us right now. Jesus promised this.

> Peace I leave with you; My (own) peace I now give and bequeath to you. Not as the world gives do I give to you. Do not let your hearts be troubled, neither let them be afraid. (Stop allowing yourselves to be agitated and disturbed; and do not permit yourselves to be fearful and intimidated and cowardly and unsettled.) (John 14:27 AMP)

The Prince of Peace has spoken. His peace is a supernatural impartation to those who believe on His Name. It is not a worldly result from practicing yoga or progressive muscle relaxation. Those avenues will relax the body but are nothing in comparison to experiencing the presence of God, which brings peace that we cannot manufacture. In this place of true focused relationship and trust, all agitation, fear, and intimidation cease to exist. Make a decision and choose to allow your mind to be filled with the truth, love, and stability of the Lord Jesus Christ.

In the end of this chapter, Jesus said Satan was coming as the time for His crucifixion drew near. He stated Satan had nothing in common with Him. He meant there was nothing in Him that belonged to Satan and that Satan had no power over Him. How then was it possible for Jesus to be crucified? This was not a passive action as some would believe.

> For this reason the Father loves Me, because I lay down My life to take it back again. No one takes it away from me. On the contrary, I lay it down voluntarily. (I put it from Myself.) I am authorized and have power to lay it down (to resign it) and I am authorized and have power to take it back again. These are the instructions (orders) which I have received (as My charge) from My Father. (John 10:17–18 AMP)

> So Pilate said to Him, Will You not speak (even) to me? Do You not know that I have power (authority) to release You and I have power to crucify You? Jesus answered, You would not have any power or authority whatsoever against (over) Me if it were not given you from above. (John 19:10–11 AMP)

Jesus displayed power in laying His life down for us. He allowed Himself to be murdered on our behalf. Through His sacrifice that which separated us from Father God was now removed forever. It is only through the broken body and shed blood of the Lord Jesus Christ that we may approach the Throne of God. Jesus dismissed His own spirit after He said it was finished. The Greek word used is "tetelestai," which is an accounting term meaning "paid in full." He actually took away our sin through His Blood. There is nothing more that needs to be done for us to be reconciled to the Father.

Depending on what has happened to you in your life, you may find it very difficult to receive the truth that Jesus redeemed you.

That is why it is so necessary to meditate upon the Word of God. I encourage you to allow God's truth, which is alive, to penetrate your mind so that you will be able to change. Find a good church and people who will love you and help you on your journey. I promise it will be so worth it. When I go home to be with Jesus in glory, my great desire is to hear Him say this to me.

"Well done, Kathi! Come celebrate with Me!"

May He smile with delight upon you and say the same.

# CHAPTER 14

## Kelsi's Writings

I found a few of Kelsi's writings in her desk several days before I finished writing the previous chapter. I thought to share them with you. You may receive something good in reading them. Some of the content is just strange; however, the final lines have haunting truth woven in.

Kelsi had written a poem several years ago entitled "Bluebloods and Flowerbuds." It was actually very good. I enjoyed how she put her thoughts together in it. Several years later, she searched but could not find it. This disturbed her a lot because she had put so much effort into it. I was disappointed too.

"Do you remember the theme you followed in the poem? What were you trying to convey?" I asked her. She brightened up and wrote down what I found in her desk in 2020. I show them as she wrote them, without making corrections.

### Bluebloods and Flowerbuds

Bluebloods and flowerbuds, how they are so unique in their own way.

Bluebloods, how they are known as the wealthy and powerful; while flowerbuds, how they bloom into the flowers they're known to be—beautiful and wonderful.

Bluebloods live in places where the wealthy and the powerful rule. They are a people who achieve so much.

Flowerbuds are the newborn flower plants that come and are ready to be born into the world to show their beauty and gracefulness.

Of course, sometimes the bluebloods can take actions that can destroy humanity and life; depending on their target.

Flowerbuds; from the day they are born, they are just young and innocent; being the way God commanded them to be.

Being a blueblood is not all bad, depending on the persons' actions. They have the power to make the world a better place, if they can just listen to truth.

All the while, flowers of nature are innocent of giving life to the world, along with beauty.

The fame and the fortune are all illusions of life; people should understand the ways of life.

So I say, to you bluebloods; learn from the flowers...

The next writing I had not seen before.

## Love

Love...
I need love
I need recognition.
I want acceptents...
I hate this loneliness...
And waiting
I can't stand it.
I sometimes fear I'll want to kill myself
How much I hate that.

I will not be tempted
I will push & push
And no one, nothing can stop me!!
The Lord says he loves me, but it still makes no
matter to me.
Will you let me live in hate?
Or show me love?

## Sunbeams and Moonbeams

Sunbeams and moonbeams, how they are
so different from each other, yet alike in a few
number of ways.

Sunbeams are from the Sun, which are
of brightening the daytime. In the rays, you
can actually see those beams, floating about in
them—the only place you can see them.

Moonbeams are from the Moon, which are
of the nighttime. In the rays, you can actually see
those beams, floating about in them—the only
place you can see them.

The sunbeams inside the rays of the rays of
the sun, are part of what the sun does; it replen-
ishes the flowers, trees, grass and so many other
plants. For the people and the animals, it gives
them light to make them happy, and alive. As
well as the need for Vitamen D.

The moonbeams inside the rays of the
moon, are part of what the moon does; it bright-
ens the night, being far more grander than its'
friends the stars. The light lets people know that
there is beauty in the nighttime; not just for
sleeping.

How people try to hold these light beams
in their hands, when they can't because all they

are there, you can't really feel them. It is all part of light.

The important thing though, is that your at least in its' glow.

## Feeling Near the Moment of Truth

I'm feeling near the moment of truth
Near the something that cannot be explained
It feels like...erratic freedom
Feels like having nothing to do about wisdom, or anything else
Almost frightening in a way
But otherwise, exhilarating

## Mermaids

Always been known and thought to be myths, mainly in those stories by sailors and drowning sailors

Until now, there is claiming of them to exist

Old fossils of very unusual creatures, with the upper body of, seemingly, human and the bottom with a tale of a fish

Footage showing such miraculous forms, and close ups to things of such possibilities

As clear as day...

The only answer is—TRUE

If there are mermaids in this world, is there, pray tell, paranormal ones, at any chance...?

Such mysteries there are of the ocean...

A real reminder of how important the ocean is a blood stream for earth

## What Is Real and What Is Not?

What is real and what is not?
People have always asked this question
Asked since, well, surely not exactly the beginning of time, but a little later off in time
In general, for most people, what is real is what we've lived with and could actually see
What is not real, usually is what we don't see
But there comes a time when we need to learn that sometimes what's real is something you can't see
And need to see it, without having to force things to come true
Like having the imagination and innocence of a child

# KATHLEEN BASEHORE

# About the Author

Kathleen Basehore is a licensed psychologist with extensive experience in the field of mental health. She has worked in direct care settings ranging from outpatient rehabilitation for the severely mentally ill to inpatient psychiatric care and then to private practice. She has pursued much psychological training in trauma and anxiety disorders. In addition, she advanced in development of spiritual modalities of inner healing prayer through Jesus Christ. Growing in love, applying principles of the Word of God to everyday life, and generational repentance enabled her to overcome previously resistant behavioral challenges. Applying cognitive behavioral techniques was another helpful avenue for change. She found joy in life even after the death of her beloved daughter in 2019.

Her daughter, Kelsi, was diagnosed with a number of psychiatric disorders at an early age. Kathleen learned how to lean into God to deal with extraordinary ongoing stressors for twenty-four years. She learned to love in the face of great pain and torment that assailed Kelsi's mind when psychiatric medications could only take the edge off.

Her first book chronicled the journey of raising Kelsi with her husband, John. That book is entitled *Can You Just... Love Her?* and is available on Amazon. You may find out more about Kathi at www. kathibasehore.com.

Motivational speaker, author, and publisher, Wendy K. Walters, reinforced her desire to write her first book. Author Teresa Parker of Sweet series fame edited that story. Their wisdom, guidance, and support laid a foundation for all works to follow.

CPSIA information can be obtained
at www.ICGtesting.com
Printed in the USA
BVHW030534061121
620521BV00003B/2